REV. JŌSHŌ ADRI

THE TRUE TEACHING ON
AMIDA BUDDHA AND HIS PURE LAND

Dharma Lion Publications

CRAIOVA, 2015

Rev. Jōshō Adrian Cîrlea (Adrian Gheorghe Cîrlea) is the representative of Jodo Shinshu Buddhist Community from Romania, founder of Tariki Dojo and Amidaji Temple.
He is also the author of *The Path of Acceptance – Commentary on Tannisho*, Dharma Lion, 2011, *Jodo Shinshu Buddhist Teachings*, Dharma Lion, 2012 and *The 48 Vows of Amida Buddha*, Dharma Lion, 2013

Cîrlea Gheorghe Adrian
Oficiul Postal 3, Ghiseul Postal 3
Casuta postala 615
Cod poştal (postal code) 200900
Craiova, judet Dolj
Romania

phone: 0725854326
e-mail: josho_adrian@yahoo.com
skype id: josho_adrian
Website:
www.amida-ji-retreat-temple-romania.blogspot.com

2

I dedicate this book to my parents and grandparents from this life (Gheorghe, Tamara, Constantin, Ioana, Gheorghe, Cristina) and other lives.
May they always have peace, love and happiness in their hearts, receive faith in Amida Buddha and be born in his Pure Land.

TABLE OF CONTENTS

FOREWORD

This book is a long term project which has begun a few years ago as a reaction to the appearance in the international sangha of some divergent views which threaten to destroy the chances of many people to listen to the genuine Amida Dharma. It is also a work in progress, and the reader can expect that I will come back again, sooner or later, with new editions and improvements.

As we all know, the Dharma is the second treasure of the The Three Treasures (Buddha, Dharma and Sangha) in which we all take refuge when we become Buddhist disciples. Simply stated, the role of the Sangha is to secure a genuine transmission of the Dharma as it was taught by Shakyamuni Buddha and the Masters of our tradition, so that we can all receive faith (shinjin) and attain Buddhahood in the Pure Land. Without such a proper transmission, there is actually no Sangha and no possibility of Liberation from birth and death, that is, no chance to become Buddhas ourselves.

More than this, the Dharma is the supreme medicine given by the Buddha, the supreme Doctor, and in receiving it we must have the attitude of humble patients whose health and salvation depend totally upon the Doctor's prescription and proper administration of the medicine. If we are priests or teachers we simply cannot be careless with people's salvation from birth and death, just like a good pharmacist does not give poison to those who come to him looking for the medicine prescribed by their doctor.

As long as we ourselves are not Doctors (Enlighted beings/Buddhas) we should also not change the Medicine (the Dharma), but instead act as the good pharmacist and give to others exactly what the Doctor has prescribed. Trully, Amida Dharma is not our property and in dealing with it, we should act only as transmitters, not creators of the teaching. This is exactly what I am trying to do in this book – to show the true teaching about Amida Buddha and His Pure Land, while also counteracting some of the most spread wrong views of our time.

Generally speaking, there are two main categories of wrong views which should be discarded by the followers of our school: 1) eternalism and 2) nihilism.

Among the first category there is the belief in an eternal creator god, while among the second category there is the denial of life after death and rebirth, as well as the denial of the actual existence of transcendent Buddhas and their realms, including Amida and His Pure Land. Both appear in various forms in the international sangha and both must be counteracted by any sincere follower, and especially by those who are responsible with the correct transmission of Amida Dharma to others. In this book, I will treat these categories of wrong views in the two parts:
1) the true teaching on Samsara and 2) the true teaching on Amida Buddha and His Pure Land.

The two parts are also inter-related with the first serving as an introduction to the second and providing some general knowledge on the samsaric worlds, karma, Buddha-nature, Nirvana, etc, that are very important in understanding the teaching on Amida Buddha and His Pure Land.

Thus, while hearing the Buddha's teaching on Samsara and the Pure Land of Enlightenment, the genuine aspiration to escape from the first and the wish to be born in the second might arise in the mind and heart of the reader. If that happens, then the efforts of writing this book were not in vain.

I am very grateful to Shaku Shinkai (Thais Campos) for proofreading the English manuscript and for providing me with valuable suggestions.

Namo Amida Butsu,
Bucharest,
Josho Adrian Cîrlea
September 16th 2559, Buddhist Era
2015 C.E.

CHAPTER I
THE TRUE TEACHING ON SAMSARA

General explanations of "being", "karma" and "rebirth"

Samsara is the cycle of repeated births and deaths through which unenlightened beings must pass due to their karmic illusions and blind passions. But before going into details on this topic, let us understand, what is a "being" or a "person", according to the Buddhist teaching, and also, what is "karma" and "rebirth"

So, dear friends, imagine you have a car in front of you. Now imagine you loose one of the wheels and you put it aside. Is the car identical with this wheel? Then take another wheel and proceed in the same way, asking yourself the same question. Continue to disassemble the car and do not stop till each component of the automobile is taken away. Now ask yourself again: do all these components taken separately represent the automobile? You will logically realize the answer is "no".

So what really is the vehicle? It is a name given to an ensemble of elements put together at a given time. What is the person (a human or non-human being) from a Buddhist point of view? An ensemble of elements gathered at a given moment. These elements are represented by ideas, sensations, feelings, thoughts, etc. All these united represent the human or non-human being. This explanation must be kept in mind if we want to understand Buddhism. The person is not something all by itself but an ensemble of various sensations, feelings, ideas, thoughts etc, united at a given moment.

The fundamental characteristic of this ensemble is transition, dynamism. When looking at a person one will see an image of this motion, an image of this ensemble in continuous movement. If one looked at that person when he/she was three years old one wouldn't have seen the same thing. This is because at that time you observed another aspect of the motion. The components of the personality would have had another aspect and a different form. After twenty years you'll see, for instance, another John, George or Mike.

Something is still preserved but at the same time something changes. I am not identical with my three year's old self, and in twenty years time I won't be completely the same with the one I am now. In Buddhism this is called the non-ego or non-self doctrine. All things exists due to causes and conditions, thus they have no nature of their own or an unchanged identity. This is why they are said to be empty. When causes and conditions come together, a certain thing exists, when they disappear, that thing also disappears. When causes and conditions change, that thing changes too.

Now let us observe another matter. What is causing this ensemble to move? Buddha's answer is: desire and craving (thirst). Our different desires and tendencies determine us to move towards one direction or another; they change our personal history and generate the karma, the action. Karma is the law of cause and effect. The term "karma" comes from the Sanskrit word "karman" which means action - acting with thought, deed and word. As a conclusion, there are three types of karma: karma of thought, of speech and karma of action or body. All that we think, speak or do will affect our personal history. What we are now represents the result of what we thought, said or did in the past, in another lifetime or in the present life; and what we think, speak and do in the present will create us in the future.

We've said that what is commonly called "person" is in continuous change and that after ten years, for example, he is not identical with the one he is today. We've said that although he is not the same, something still remains; well, this something is the causal continuity. When a man sets a stack on fire and the fire extends to the whole village and burns down the house of another peasant situated at the opposite side of the village, the first peasant could say that he has nothing to do with this disaster, for the fire which burnt the house of the second peasant is not identical with the flame he used for setting his straws on fire. But there is a causal continuity between the first fire and the one which burnt the second peasant's house. This is how things are concerning the karma. The ensemble in continuous motion, that is the human or non-human being, is moved by a desire which generates karma. We are the result of our own karma.

11

Karma may last forever and determines our birth in another life. So we have arrived to what is called "reincarnation". But from the Buddhist point of view a more appropriate word would be **rebirth**. When using the term "reincarnation", the idea implied in it is that there would be a self dependent, unchangeable thing which passes from one body to another. But we have underlined in our presentation that the ensemble named "person" is in continuous motion and transformation, which is why the term "mind-stream" is often used in the Buddhist texts to emphasize this constant changing. So, we see that the word **rebirth** is more adequate. A man in his daily life dies and is reborn permanently, according to the changes, the tendencies and the desires which occur in his mind-stream and the physical body[1]. We've given earlier the example with the age of three years and twenty years.

In the moment of death, our personal karma determines the form and the vehicle, that is, the body which the mind-stream will have in the next birth. Our desires need a vehicle to follow them and fulfill them in another life. The environment where we will be born in another life and the shape we will have, depend on the karma. Buddha states that not even a single man can escape his karma:

"Not in the heaven, not in the middle of the ocean, not in the mountain caves: there is no place in this world were you can hide from the consequences of your deeds."

The doctrine of karma teaches us that we are completely responsible of what we are and of what we will become. Nobody besides us, be it a god, human or any other being, can be held responsible. We deserve what happens to us, even if it is hard to accept that.

---

1 Physically, our cells change every seven years, so we are not even physically the same.

There is no supreme god or creator in the Buddha Dharma

Nowadays, many people from inside or outside the Sangha spread the idea that Shakyamuni Buddha did not deny nor affirm the existence of God. Thus, they somehow imply that the World Honored One left the door open for interpretation and that it is ok for a Buddhist disciple to believe in a Creator or supreme God.

Well, this is a great delusion and a falsification of Shakyamuni's teaching. In fact, the Buddha clearly denied the existence of a supreme being who created the world, rules the world and will one day judge the world. In this short chapter I do not have the intention to enter into any debate or polemics with followers of other religions on the existence or non-existence of such a supreme being, but just to prove that Shakyamuni Buddha clearly denied this view and considered it a false and dangerous illusion. For me the most important thing is not what monotheistic religions say, or if some chose to believe in a creator god (its their choice), but what the Buddha actually said and preached. So, if we consider ourselves to be His diciples, we ought to know His position on this topic and follow it faithfully.

It is well known that among the many religious and philosophical traditions that were contemporary with the Buddha, the idea of a supreme being who created and sustains the world was well known and shared by many. This is exactly why, He did not keep silence, but preached against it.

In the *Discourse on Brahma's Invitation* (*Brahmanimantanika Sutra*) [2], Buddha tells the story of His visit to the heavenly place of a

---

[2] The *Brahmanimantanika Sutra*, which is a part of *Majjhima Nikaya* 49 has a parallel in the *Madhyama Āgama* (MĀ 78), which agrees with the Pali version in its title of *"Brahma inviting the Buddha"* (梵天請佛), and also that the Buddha is staying at Jeta's forest near Savatthī. The first part of the *Brahmanimantanika Sutra* appears as a discourse in the Samyutta Nikaya and is called the *Brahma Baka Sutra*

powerful god, called Baka Brahma, to convince him to renounce to his wrong view about himself and his realm:

"Bhikshus[3], once I was staying at the foot of a royal sal tree in the Subhaga Grove at Ukattha. Now at that time, an evil wrong view had arisen in the Brahma Baka thus:

'This Brahma realm is permanent; this is everlasting; this is eternal; this is everything [complete in itself]; this is not subject to passing away, nor is this born, nor does it decay, nor die, nor pass away (from the heavens), nor is reborn; and there is also no escape beyond this.'
Having known with my mind the thought in the Brahma Baka's mind, just as a strong man would stretch his bent arm or would bend his stretched arm, I vanished from the foot of the royal sal tree in the Subhaga Grove at Ukattha and reappeared in the Brahma world".

Seeing Him coming, the Baka Brahma confirms to the Blessed One that he indeed shared that view:

"Now, good sir, this Brahma realm is permanent; this is everlasting; this is eternal; this is everything [complete in itself]; this is not subject to passing away, nor is this born, nor does it decay, nor

---

(S 6.4).3 All three versions open with Baka believing his realm to be permanent and supreme, and the Buddha, aware of this wrong view, thereupon visits him.
Apparently, the *Brahmanimantanika Sutra* is an expansion of the account of the *Brahma Baka Sutra* (S 6.4), or that the latter, giving only a brief account, is a summary of the former. More likely, however, both texts were built on an ur-text (common original text). Both the sutta openings are identical, but while the *Brahmanimantanika Sutra* is set at Ukkattha, the *Brahma Baka Sutra* is set at Sarvasti. It is also interesting to note that the Majjhima account is given in the first person, with the Buddha himself narrating the event, but the Samyutta account is in the third person. Both the *Brahma Baka Sutra* (S 6.4) and the MĀ 78 version agree in saying that the Buddha is residing in Jeta's forest near Savatthī. Moreover, this account recurs in the *Baka Brahma Jataka*.
(Introduction to the English version of the *Brahmanimantanika Sutta* by Piya Tan). The passages quoted in this subchapter are mainly from the translation made by Piya Tan, with the exception indicated in the respective footnote.
[3] Bhiksus means "monks". Shakyamuni begins this sutra (discourse) by addressing directly to the monks by his own accord. It is something like, "dear monks…".

die, nor pass away (from the heavens), nor is reborn; and there is also no escape beyond this.'"

Hearing this, Shakyamuni immediately tried to correct him by stating that nothing is really permanent or eternal, not even the realm and power of the gods:

"Alas! The worthy Brahma Baka has fallen into ignorance in that he says of the impermanent that it is permanent; of the non-everlasting that it is everlasting; of the non-eternal that it is eternal; of the incomplete that it is everything; of what is subject to passing away as being not subject to passing away; of where one is born, and decays, and dies, and passes away (from the heavens), and is reborn, that this is where one is not subject to passing away, nor is born, nor decays, nor dies, nor passes away (from the heavens), nor is reborn; and when there is an escape beyond this, he says that there is no escape beyond this.'"

But then, to prevent the Buddha from stating more truths, the demon Mara[4] possessed a member of Baka Brahma's host and entered the discussion by addressing the Buddha with the term "bhiksu" (monk), like He was just an ordinary seeker, inferior to Brahma:

---

[4] The *Nirvana Sutra* lists four types of demons: 1) greed, anger and delusion; 2) the five skandas, or obstructions caused by physical and mental functions; 3) death; and 4) the demon of the Heaven of Free Enjoyment of Manifestations by Others (Paranirmitavaśavartin). So, in the Buddhist texts the word "demon" is sometimes used with the meaning of internal demons, or personal blind passions and illusions, but also in the sense of an actually existing being or beings that disturb others from reaching freedom from birth and death. Nowadays, there is a common mistake among many so called "modern" Buddhists, who think that maras are only internal and not external demons, too. However, I encourage my Dharma friends and readers to please not share in their misunderstandings, and single-heartedly entrust to Amida Buddha, which is the best way to be protected against the influence of such evil and powerful beings.

"Then Mara, the evil one, possessed a certain member of Brahma's host[5], and he told me:
'Bhikshu, bhikshu, do not disparage him, do not disparage him. For this Brahma is the Great Brahmā, the Conqueror, the Unconquered, the Omniscient, the Omnipotent, the Lord God, the Maker, the Creator, the Chief, the Ordainer, the Almighty, the Father of all that are and that will be."

This passage is extremely important as it shows the delusion Mara tries to offer to the god Brahma and to all beings – the so called existence of a supreme creator god who rules everything. Thus, he mentions some of the titles that nowadays monotheistic religions apply to their so called "supreme god": *"the Omniscient, the Omnipotent, the Lord God, the Maker, the Creator, the Chief, the Ordainer, the Almighty, the Father of all that are and that will be."*

In his efforts to impose this wrong view, he tries to frighten the audience by saying that before Shakyamuni, there were many other *"recluses and brahmins"* who were against this supreme creator god and who, after death, were reborn in the lower realms[6] for their lack of faith, while others who had faith and praised the Brahma, acquired a superior rebirth and body[7]. Then, he urges the Buddha to obey this supreme Brahma and do not go against him:

---

[5] It should be noted here that Mara is simply using this *"certain member of Brahma's host"* clearly as a fifth columnist. In fact, Mara has completely overpowered Brahma, Brahma's host and Brahma's retinue. (Translator's note).

[6] *"Before your time, bhikshu, there were recluses and brahmins in the world who scorned earth, loathed earth; who scorned water, loathed water; who scorned fire, loathed fire; who scorned air [wind], loathed air [wind]; who scorned beings, loathed beings; who scorned gods, loathed gods; who scorned Prajapati, loathed Prajapati; who scorned Brahma, loathed Brahma; and when the body had broken up after their breath was cut off, they were established in an inferior body."*

[7] *"Before your time, bhikshu, there also were recluses and brahmins in the world who lauded earth, delighted in earth; who lauded water, delighted in water; who lauded fire, delighted in fire; who lauded air, delighted in air; who lauded beings, delighted in beings; who lauded gods, delighted in gods; who lauded Prajapati, delighted in Prajapati; who lauded Brahma, delighted in Brahma; and when the body had broken up after their breath was cut off, they were established in a superior body."*

"So, bhikshu, I tell you this:

'Come now, good sir, do only as Brahma says! Go not against the word of Brahma. If you go against the word of Brahma, bhikshu, then, you would be like a man trying to deflect approaching glory with a stick, or, bhikshu, you would be like a man losing his hold of earth with his hand and feet as he falls down the deep chasm—so it will be unto you, bhikshu.

Come now, good sir, do only as Brahma God says! Go not against the word of Brahma. Do you not see Brahma's host seated here, bhikshu?' And then Mara the evil one led me up close to Brahma's host."

But the Buddha immediately recognized Mara under the disguise of a member in Brahma's host, and exposed his treachery to all. Unfortunately, He was the only one there who had not fallen under Maras's influence:

"When this was said, I told this to Mara the evil one:

'I know you, evil one. Do not think, "He does not know." You are Mara the evil one, and Brahma and Brahma's host and Brahma's retinue have all fallen into your hands; they have fallen under your power. You, evil one, think, 'This world has fallen into my hands! He [the Buddha], too, has fallen under my power!' But I have not fallen into your hands, evil one; I have not fallen under your power!'"

Thus, when Baka Brahma enters again in the discussions he does so only to re-assert his wrong views I mentioned above, at the beginning of this article. Then, filled with his godly pride he threatens the Buddha, trying to bring Him into submission:

"Bhikshu, I tell you this: You will find no escape beyond, and you will only reap your share of toil and trouble" but […] *"if you will hold on to Brahma [God], you will be close to me, rest in my domain, so that I may work my will upon you and make you low and humble."*

Not afraid, the Buddha speaks about the limitations of Brahma, proving to him that even if he now has (due to his previous karma) great power over a very large part of the universe, and knows everything high and low in it, still there are places of existence which

17

are not under his domain, and gods (themselves unenlightened and not supreme) far more superior than him:

"I know your destiny (karma), Brahma, and I know your splendor [your fall]".
As far as the sun and moon course their way, lighting the quarters with their radiance,
Over that thousandfold world, your might hold sway.
There you know the high and low, and the lustful and the lust free,
Such and such existences, the comings and goings of beings.

"Thus, Brahma, I know your reach and I know your radiance: the Brahma Baka has this much might, the Brahma Baka has this much power, the Brahma Baka has this much sway. But, Brahma, there are three other bodies and worlds[8], that you neither know nor see; but which I know and see.

Thus, the Buddha relates to him that his present situation is in fact, an involution from higher states where he once dwelt. **As everything that goes up must one day fall, Baka Brahma too, fell from previous better realms when the good karma that brought him there was exhausted.** Unfortunately, due to his ignorance and limited power he cannot remember them, but the Enlightenment's vision being all-pervading, the Buddha can see them:

"(1) There is, Brahma, the world called Ābhāsvara (Heaven of Supreme Light)[9], having arisen here, you fell from it. Because you have dwelt here for so long, your memory has lapsed, and so you neither know nor see it, but I know and see it. As such, Brahma, as regards direct knowledge, you and I are not of the same level at all, for how could I know less? Rather, I know more than you.

---

[8] These are the second Dhyana Heaven, the third Dhyana Heaven and the fourth Dhyana Heaven in the World of Form, together with their respective realms and beings. They are situated above the first Dhyana Heaven with its three realms, which is the only one ruled by Baka Brahma.
[9] The greatest realm in the second Dhyana Heaven.

18

(2) There is, Brahma, the world called Śubhakrtsna (Heaven of Universal Purity)[10], having arisen here, you fell from it. Because you have dwelt here for so long, your memory has lapsed, and so you neither know nor see it, but I know and see it. As such, Brahma, as regards direct knowledge, you and I are not of the same level at all, for how could I know less? Rather, I know more than you.

(3) There is, Brahma, the world called Brhatphala (Heaven of Greater Fruits)[11], that you neither know nor see. I know and see it. As such, Brahma, as regards direct knowledge, you and I are not of the same level at all, for how could I know less? Rather, I know more than you."

Then, in order to prove the limitations of Brahma, the Buddha challenged him to see who among them can vanish from each other's sight:

"'Well then, good sir, I will disappear from you.'
"'Well then, Brahma, disappear from me if you can.'"[12]

Of course, Brahma was unable to prove his superiority and could not hide himself from the Buddha's unimpeded vision:

"Then Baka Brahma, [thinking,] 'I will disappear from Gotama the contemplative. I will disappear from Gotama the contemplative,' was not able to disappear from me.[13]

As for the Buddha, this was not a difficult thing to do, and so he disappeared from Brahma and his retinue's sight, allowing them to only hear His voice[14]:

---

[10] The greatest realm in the third Dhyana Heaven.

[11] The third realm in the fourth Dhyana Heaven.

[12] *"Brahma-nimantanika Sutta: The Brahma Invitation"* (MN 49), translated from the Pali by Thanissaro Bhikkhu. Access to Insight (Legacy Edition), 17 December 2013, http://www.accesstoinsight.org/tipitaka/mn/mn.049.than.html

[13] *"Brahma-nimantanika Sutta: The Brahma Invitation"* (MN 49), translated from the Pali by Thanissaro Bhikkhu. Access to Insight (Legacy Edition), 17 December 2013, http://www.accesstoinsight.org/tipitaka/mn/mn.049.than.html

"So then, bhikshus, I fabricated a fabrication of psychic power to the extent that Brahma, the Brahma assembly, and the attendants of the Brahma assembly heard my voice but did not see me. Having disappeared, I recited this verse:

'Having seen
danger
right in becoming,
and becoming
searching for non-becoming,
I didn't affirm
any kind of becoming,
or cling to any delight.'"[15]

This amazes Brahma and his retinue who start to recognize Buddha's superiority, but Mara again quickly intervenes and tries to convince Buddha to give up the teaching of such ideas, and to not accept disciples:

"Then Mara the evil one possessed a certain member of Brahma's host, and he told me:
'Good sir, if that is what you know, if that is what you have understood, do not guide your disciples and renunciants! Do not teach the Dharma to your disciples and renunciants!"

Again, he tries to frighten the Buddha by saying that those renunciants and spiritual seekers who did like Him and preached such

---

[14] *Idem.*

[15] "In other words, the act of searching for non-becoming — or annihilation — is also a type of becoming. Although the Buddhist path aims at the cessation of becoming*(bhava),* it does not attempt this cessation by trying to annihilate the process of becoming. Instead, it does so by focusing on what has already come to be *(bhuta),*developing dispassion for what has come to be and for the nutriment — the causes — of what has come to be. With no more passion, there is no clinging to or taking sustenance from the causes of what has come to be. And through this lack of clinging or sustenance comes release". Footnote 10, from *"Brahma-nimantanika Sutta: The Brahma Invitation"* (MN 49), translated from the Pali by Thanissaro Bhikkhu. Access to Insight (Legacy Edition), 17 December 2013, http://www.accesstoinsight.org/tipitaka/mn/mn.049.than.html

ideas were reborn in lower states[16], while those who abstained and kept to themselves, had a good rebirth[17].

But the Buddha reveals the wicked intentions of Mara:

*"'I know you, evil one. Do not think, "He does not know." You are Mara the evil one! It is not out of compassion for their welfare that you speak thus. It is without compassion for their welfare that you speak thus. You think thus, evil one: **'Those to whom the recluse Gotama teaches the Dharma will escape from my sphere!'**"'*

So, this is the reason why Mara tried to prevent the Buddha to teach the non-existence of a creator god, all powerful and eternal, because such a teaching would free people from his influence. In this sutra, Mara is thus regarded not only as the celestial demon of the Heaven of Free Enjoyment of Manifestations by Others (Paranirmitavaśavartin), but also as impersonating delusion, ignorance and all the internal and external obstacles that prevent Enlightenment. Thus, according to the Buddha, **the belief in a supreme god, creator and sustainer of the universe, is a grave error and an obstacle to true freedom from the repeated cycle of birth and death**.

In contrast to the various renunciants or spiritual seekers, who believed in the eternal god creator Brahma, or those that Mara gave as an example before, the Buddha is a truly Awakened One:

---

[16] *"Before your time, bhikshu, there were recluses and brahmins in the world claiming to be worthy and fully self-awakened, and they guided their disciples and renunciants. They taught the Dharma to their disciples and renunciants. They craved for disciples and renunciants. And when the body had broken up after their breath was cut off, they were established in an inferior body".*

[17] *"Before your time, bhikshu, there were also recluses and brahmins in the world claiming to be worth and fully self-awakened, and they did not guide their disciples and renunciants. They did not teach the Dharma to their disciples and renunciants. They had no craving for disciples and renunciants. And when the body had broken up after their breath was cut off, they were established in a superior body. So, bhikshu, I tell you this. Good sir, dwell unconcerned, devoted to a pleasant abiding here and now. It is wholesome [It is better] to leave it undeclared, good sir, do not advise anyone!'"*

"Those recluses and brahmins of yours, evil one, who claimed to be fully self-awakened were not fully self-awakened. But I, who claim to be fully self-awakened, am (truly) fully self-awakened.

[...] Evil one, the Tathagata has abandoned the mental influxes that defile, bring renewal of being, give trouble, ripen in suffering, and lead to further birth, decay and death. Evil one, He has cut them off at the root, made them like a palm-tree stump, done away with them so that they are not subject to further growth. In this manner, evil one, the Tathagata has abandoned the mental influxes that defile, cut them off at the root, made them like a palm-tree stump, done away with them so that they are not subject to further growth.'"

There are also other discourses in which Shakyamuni Buddha clearly denied the existence of a supreme god, and I plan to show them to you in my next articles in this category. Now, I just wish to insist a little more upon the situation described above. What we see in the sutra, is a powerful god, possessing a very long life due to his previous good karma from the past, who falls in the delusion that he is supreme in the universe and also the creator and master of the world. And the one who supports him in this deluded idea is the most powerful demon of samsara – Mara, the evil one. If we somehow place the story of the *Brahmanimantanika Sutra* in modern context and relate it to the monotheistic religions of nowadays, we can say their supreme god is under the influence of Satan who fooled him into believing that he is: *"the Omniscient, the Omnipotent, the Lord God, the Maker, the Creator, the Chief, the Ordainer, the Almighty, the Father of all that are and that will be."* This should make all those who have the tendency to mix Buddhism with Christianity or other monotheistic religions to think twice before making their wrong assumption that the Buddha did not deny the existence of a supreme/creator god. If we carefully read the passages above from the *Brahmanimantanika Sutra* and other discourses, we clearly see that there is no place in the Buddhist thought for the actual existence of a supreme/creator being.

Of course, there are many powerful gods, ruling over vast realms of samsara, who might have the delusion of being supreme and eternal, just like many humans declare themselves supreme among their kind, but this is just one delusion among the many delusions of the unenlightened beings. In truth, the prosperity, lifespan, power and abilities, as well as the realms and forms in which we are born are due to our karma, and will change according to karma. Nothing is enduring for ever, and those who are now in a position of great strength in human world or celestial worlds, will one day fall, when the karma for being there will be exhausted. Thus, even the most powerful gods die. To have faith in one of them, especially in those who have the delusion that they are all-powerful, may be beneficial in short term, and even lead to rebirth in their heavenly realms, if we also cultivate good deeds, but in long term, when those gods and their realms disappear, or when our karma for being there also comes to an end, we'll fall again in the lower realms. This is why only the state of Buddhahood or Nirvana should be our single goal in the religious life, because there is no decay and fall from it:

"The enlightenment of nonbuddhist ways is called impermanent, Buddhist Enlightenment is called eternal. The emancipation of nonbuddhist ways is called impermanent, the Emancipation of Buddhist ways is called eternal".[18]

---

[18] Passage from the *Nirvana Sutra,* quoted by Shinran Shonin in his *Kyogyoshinsho*, chapter V. *The Collected Works of Shinran*, Shin Buddhism Translation Series, Jodo Shinshu Hongwanji-ha, Kyoto, 1997, p.505.p.182

Some Buddhist explanations on the origin and existence of the universe

Regard this phantom world
As a star at dawn, a bubble in a stream,
A flash of lightning in a summer cloud
A flickering lamp — a phantom — and a dream.

Shakyamuni Buddha

Question: If the Buddha Dharma denies the idea of a creator god, then how does it explain the existence of the various worlds and universes?

First of all, when it refers to worlds and universes, the Buddha Dharma explains them as places of rebirth, or Samsaric realms. Thus, they are inhabited by unenlightened beings in various stages of spiritual evolution or involution. As far as I know, most of the monotheists give the following argument in the support of their belief in a supreme creator-god: "if you see a house in a field you ask yourself who built it. In the same way, this complex world is the creation of our god. Anything that exists has a creator". This is the basis of their belief system, but for Buddhists the matter is wrongly addressed here. Yes, indeed, everything has a creator, but not in the way the monotheists think. I would rather say, **every dream has a creator – the dreamer**. And who is the dreamer? It is us – the unenlightened beings with our specific individual karma, but also with the collective karma or the karmic connections we create among us.

The various worlds and universes are intrinsically linked with the beings who inhabit them. So, we can say that the first exist because of the karma of unenlightened beings or in other words, the karma of unenlightened beings is the primary cause for the existence of worlds and universes. Let's take a look, for example, to the hell realms. Who are the tormentors, "hell wardens" or terrifying beasts who apply punishment to those born there? What is the true nature of the molten bronze, of the fierce mountains, rivers of fire, and various other material elements which are to be found in hells[19]? Are they created by somebody, and do they have an existence of their own? According

---

[19] There are **Eight Hot Hells** and **Eight Cold Hells** which are described as one on top of the other like stores of a building. The **Eight Hot Hells** are: 1. Hell of Repetition or the Reviving Hell, where inhabitants see each other as mortal enemies and fight with each other with huge and inconceivable weapons created by their karma, until everyone is cut into pieces; then, when they all lie dead, a voice from the sky of that hell says: "Revive!" and they immediately come back to life and restart their fight; 2. Hell of the Black Rope, where beings are seized by the hell wardens, laid down on the ground made of burning metal and marked with *"hot iron cords in both directions as a carpenter makes marks with his line" (Ojoyoshu)* after which they are cut into pieces with burning saws and iron axes or disemboweled with swords along these lines, only to become whole once more and the process repeats itself over and over again; 3. Hell of Assembly or the Rounding-Up and Crushing Hell, where beings are crushed by pairs of huge mountains or by the flaming heads of various animals which the hell-beings have killed in their past lives and who now throw themselves into one another, catching the poor people in the middle and crushing them to death; 4. Hell of Lamentations, where beings are roasted in buildings of hot metal with no exit, or they are boiled and poured molten copper into their mouths which burns up their internal organs; 5. Hell of Great Lamentations, where the wardens put a multitude of victims into metal sheds with double walls blazing with fire and as the doors are all sealed, the beings there howl in pain thinking that even if they succeed in getting past the first door, they cannot get through the second; 6. Hell of Scorching Heat, where beings suffer by being cooked in huge iron cauldrons filled with molten bronze, and whenever they surface, they are grabbed by the hell wardens with metal hooks and beaten in the head with hammers until they lose consciousness; 7. Hell of the Great Scorching Heat, where beings are blocked inside blazing metal houses where hell wardens impale them through their heels and the anus with tridents of hot iron until the prongs push out through the shoulders and the top of the head; and 8. Hell of Suffering without Interruption (Avici), where all the torments of the previous hells are experienced in more horrific ways and without interruption.

The **Eight Cold Hells** are located on the same level as the Eight Hot Hells, but in comparison with them, where fire is dominant, here the karmic environment is composed of snow mountains and glaciers, and the winds are ravaging blizzards. These hells are: 1. Hell of Blisters (Arbuda), where various ice blisters erupt on the body of the beings while they are submerged in extremely cold water or blasted by the wind; 2. Hell of Burst Blisters (Nirarbuda), where the blisters become open sores; 3. Hell of Clenched Teeth (Atata), where the teeth of the beings are tightly clenched due to extreme cold; 4. Hell of Lamentation (Hahava), where the beings greatly lament while their tongues are paralyzed and find it difficult to breathe or scream; 5. Hell of Groans (Huhuva), where the voices of beings are cracked and long groans escape from their lips; 6. Hell of Utpala-like Cracks (Utpala) or the

to the Buddhist teaching they are the manifestation of the evil karma of the hell dwellers[20], just like the monsters and terrifying places in our nightmares are created by our own thoughts and cravings. In the nightmares, the monsters and the terrifying places are real for the dreamer, and it is exactly so for those reborn in hells.

Thus, there is no creator god who made hell or invented the "hell wardens" to punish the sinners, because the sinners themselves are responsible for the existence of those places. Every thought and action we do is a cause that will have consequences (effects). If we constantly dwell on evil thoughts and deeds, we change our inner world (our mind stream) and we'll sooner or later be surrounded by

---

Blue Flower Hell, where the skin of beings born there is blue and splits into four petals-like pieces; 7. Hell of Lotus-like Cracks (Padma) or the Lotus Flower Hell, where the red raw flesh of beings becomes visible, and the cold makes it split into eight pieces, which makes it look like a lotus flower; 8. Hell of Great Lotus-like Cracks (Mahapadma) or the Great Lotus Hell, where the beings flesh turns dark red and splits into sixteen, thirty-two and then into innumerable pieces, thus looking like a large lotus flower; also various worms penetrate the cracked flesh and devour it with their metal beaks.

According to Shakyamuni, and various Buddhist masters who explained them, the Eight Hot Hells have their own adjacent or **neighboring hells** (utsadas):

"There are eight hells there that I have revealed, difficult to get out of, full of cruel beings, each
having sixteen utsadas (neighboring hells); they have four walls and four gates;
they are as high as they are wide; they are encircled by walls of fire; their ceiling is
fire; their sun is burning, sparkling fire; and they are filled with flames hundreds of
yojanas high." (Bodhisattva Vasubandhu, *Abhidharmakosabhasyam*)

Other types of hell are also the **temporary hells** (pradesikanakara in Skt), which were created through the actions of one being, two beings, or many beings. As Bodhisattva Vasubandhu explains, their variety is great and their place is not fixed, so they can be found in rivers, mountains, deserts, and elsewhere:

"There are the pradesika (ephemeral) hells, created through the force of individual actions, the actions of one being, of two beings, of many beings. Their variety is great; their place is not determined: river, mountain, desert, and elsewhere". (Abhidharmakosabhasyam)

[20] Bodhisattva Vasubandhu, the 2nd Patriarch of Jodo Shinshu, also explained this in the 4th stanza of his *Vijnaptimatravimsaka* and he stated the same in his *Abhidharmakosabhasyam*.

an evil and painful outside world (our bodies and the environment). So, after we leave this human form and world, we'll be reborn in a body and world that will correspond with (is a reflection of) our minds and karma.

Just like hells are the reflection of the most evil karma of beings, the rest of the planes of existence (animals[21], hungry ghosts, humans, asuras or demigods, and gods), also appear due to the karma of beings.

Thus, we can say that the six realms of existence, which are described in the sacred texts, are, on one hand, six dimensions of consciousness or six dimensions of possible experiences which manifests in us, individually, as the six negative emotions (anger/hate, greed, ignorance, jealousy, pride and pleasurable distraction[22]), and on the other hand, they are actual realms into which beings are born due to collective karma.

Even while living in our human bodies, we are connected to each realm/dimension and we have in us the seeds of rebirth into every one of them. Thus, during our lifetime, when we experience different emotions, we participate in some of the characteristic qualities and

---

[21] Animals live in various places, not just in the human world, and they suffer from both eating one another, and from exploitation. They are hunted or raised for their meat and various products of their bodies, thus experiencing inconceivable torments, and almost none of them dying a natural death.
Bodhisattva Nagarjuna lamented the state of animals in the following verses:
"Even when in the state of an animal rebirth,
there are all sorts of sufferings:
Being slaughtered, tied up, being beaten, and so on.
For those who've had to give up (the ability for) constructive behavior
leading to (a state of) peace,
There's the extremely unbearable devouring of one another".

Some are killed for the sake of (their) pearls or wool,
Or bones, meat, or pelts;
While others, being powerless, are forced into servitude,
Beaten with kicks, fists, or whips, or with hooks or with prods

(Verses 89 and 90 from *Letter to a Friend* (bShes-pa'i springs-yig, Skt. Suhrllekha) by Nagarjuna, translated by Alexander Berzin, 2006)
[22] Pleasurable distraction is the emotional state when the other five emotions are present in equal measure, harmoniously balanced.

suffering predominant in other realms. For example, when we are dominated by hate and anger we are like the hell beings, when we are greedy we feel something similar with those born in the hungry ghost realm (pretas)[23], whose bodies are tormented by insatiable thirst or hunger; when we think only to satisfy our sexual desires, we resemble animals; when we are filled with pride, we enjoy and suffer

---

[23] There are two kinds of pretas (hungry ghosts): **1. pretas who live collectively**, and **2. pretas who travel through space**. Among the pretas who live collectively, there are three types: the pretas who suffer from external obscurations, pretas who suffer from internal obscurations and pretas who suffer from specific obscurations.

Pretas who suffer from external obscurations are the pretas who suffer from intense hunger and thirst or from unbearable heat and cold. Thus, whatever food or water they see in the distance, it proves to be nothing but a mirage, because when they come closer, they realize it vanished, dried up or that it is guarded by armed demons who beat them and chase them away.

Pretas who suffer from internal obscurations have very small mouths, some no bigger than the eye of a needle, and a large sized stomach of hundreds of meters or even more. When they try to drink water, the heat of their breath evaporates it as soon as it goes down their throats. In the same way, no matter how much they eat, they cannot be satisfied due to the contradiction between their mouths and stomachs, but even if they somehow manage to eat a little, it will burst into flames during the night and burn their inside organs. Also movement is extremely hard and painful to them because of their grass-like limbs.

Pretas who suffer from specific obscurations vary from one another, according to the specific causes that brought them into that state. For example, some have many creatures living on their bodies and devouring them, or may have their own food transformed into various uneatable and foul matters, while some other cut their own flesh and eat it.

Pretas who travel through space are various types of pretas which are generaly tormented by constant fear and hallucination. Generaly speaking, they want to offload their pain on others, so wherever they go they do harm to others, so many of them fall into hells when their life as a preta comes to an end. Even when they visit their relatives from previous life, they bring only sickness, insanity and various other sufferings. They also suffer from the distorted perceptions of other kind of pretas, like perceiving the sun of winter to be too cold, or the moon too hot in summer night. Their bodily form may be of various hideous animals, like ugly dogs, birds and others.

just like the asuras (demigods)[24] who are always prone to fighting. When we try hard to cultivate moral discipline, but still can't give up jealousy as the dominant emotion, we may be reborn mentally or physically in the human world[25]. Also, when the five negative

---

[24] Although the Asuras experience various pleasures and abundance which are far superior to those of humans, and even rival those of the gods, they are constantly tormented by pride, quarreling and fighting. Beings in the human realm who are more spiritually advanced than others, but who strongly manifest these characteristics will be born among the Asuras. In their own realm, Asuras divide themselves in various groups and territories and fight never ending wars, while also, because they envy the pleasures of the lower realms of the gods, start useless conflicts with them, which they eventually lose.

In some texts, the realm of Asuras is counted among the lower gods, because of the pleasures found there, or among the lower realms, together with hells, animals, and pretas, because of the pain they inflict to themselves. In conclusion, life as an Asura is a pitiful one – filled as it is with joys and pleasures more than a human can imagine, but not being capable to enjoy it due to envy, pride and conflicts.

[25] Life in human form does not contain so much suffering like in the hells, pretas and animal realms, but contains less happiness than in the asura and gods realms. Because of this, even if it has its own disadvantages, the human realm is the most desirable place of birth, from the spiritual point of view. Buddhas themselves, when appearing in the world to turn the wheel of Dharma, they do so in human form.

To illustrate the extreme difficulty of rebirth in the human realm, as opposed to the lower realms, Shakyamuni Buddha compared it to the likelihood that a blind turtle, surfacing from the depths of the ocean only once every one hundred years, would encounter a tree trunk with a hole suitable for nesting:

"Sooner, do I declare, would a one-eyed turtle, if he were to pop up to the surface of the sea only once at the end of every hundred years, chance to push his neck through a yoke with one hole than would a fool, who has once gone to the three lower realms, be reborn as a man."
(Samyutta Nikaya. v. 455)

The sacred texts often insists that we should appreciate the rare chance of birth in human form and do whatever we can to put it to good use for Dharma practice:

"Hard is it to be born into human life, now we are living it. Difficult is it to hear the teachings of the Blessed One, now we hear it. Even through ages of myriads of kalpas, hard is it to hear such an excellent, profound, and wonderful doctrine. Now we are able to hear and receive it. Let us thoroughly understand the true meaning of Tathagata's teaching".

emotions (anger/hate, greed, ignorance, jealousy, pride) are to be found in balance and low quantity (this is what is meant by "pleasurable distraction"), and we try even harder to accumulate good karma, we may feel like those reborn among the gods of the world of desire[26], and after death we will actually go there. If we try hard to

---

However, human beings, afflicted as they are with the Eight Sufferings, namely, birth, old age, disease, death, separation from loved ones, meeting with the people they hate, unfulfilled wishes and the suffering associated with the five skandas (1. form, 2. perception, 3. conceptions and ideas, 4. volition and 5. conscience or mind.), find it very hard to have a true spiritual evolution. They are born in pain, have a fragile body when compared with that of many other beings, and generally speaking, their lifespan is not definite, as death may come anytime to young and old alike. Also, their experience is contradictory, changing quickly from pleasant to painful, and thus, nothing is truly certain in the human realm. Because of these conditions inherent in human beings, they often lose the rare chance they have and fall again to the lower realms.

[26] In the **World of Desire (Kamadhatu)**, there are six classes of gods with their specific realms.

The first realm is the Heaven of the Four Kings (Caturmaharaja),. As Master Genshin explained, *"one day and night in the realm of the Four Kings is as long as fifty years of human life, and life in the realm of the Four Kings lasts five hundred years"*.

The second realm is the Heaven of the Thirty-three Gods (Trayastrimsa). The most important god of this realm is Sakra (or Indra in some texts).
As Master Genshin explained, *"a hundred years of human life are equal in length to one day and night in the Heaven of the Thirty-three, and in this heaven life lasts a thousand years"*.

The third realm is the Heaven of Good Time (Yama or Suyama).
As Master Genshin explained, *"two hundred years of human life are equal in length to one day and night in Heaven of Yama, where life lasts two thousand years"*.

The fourth realm is the Heaven of Contentment (Tusita).
Queen Maya, the mother of Shakyamuni Buddha was reborn there when she died, seven days after giving birth to him. During his earthly life, Shakyamuni often made visits to this realm (and other heavenly realms, too) in order to teach the Dharma to His mother and the gods living there.
As Master Genshin explained, *"four hundred years of human life are equal in length to one day and night in Tusita, and in this heaven life continues for four thousand years"*.

practice various kinds of Samadhi and meditation we can also enjoy pleasures that go higher than material desires, and so after death we can advance to the gods living in the world of form[27] (which is higher than the world of desire) and even further to the gods in the world of non-form[28], who do not have any attachment to body, and do not even possess a definite body.

The fifth realm is the Heaven of Enjoyment of Pleasures Provided by Themselves (Nirmanarati).
As Master Genshin explained, *"eight hundred years of human life are equal in length to one day and night in Nirmanarati, where life lasts eight thousand years"*.

The sixth realm is the Heaven of Free Enjoyment of Manifestations by Others (Paranirmitavasavartin).
This realm is inhabited by Maras, the celestial demons who usually go to the other worlds to obstruct practitioners from advancing on the Buddhist Path. The karma they accumulated in past lives was good enough to make them reborn in this high heaven, but still, their lust for power and their selfishness, which were not eradicated, transformed them into living obstacles for other beings. Thus, they do everything in their power so that nobody gets higher than their plane of existence.

[27] In the **World of Form (Rupadhatu)** there are four spheres of heavenly realms, as follows:
The First Dhyana, which contains, 1. Heaven of the Councilors of Brahma (Brahmaparisadya), 2. Heaven of the High Priests of Brahma (Brahmapurohita), 3. Heaven of Great Brahma (Mahabrahman) – this is where Baka Brahma, the god who was under the illusion that he is supreme in the world, was dwelling.

The Second Dhyana, which contains, 1. Heaven of Lesser Light (Parītta-ābha), 2. Heaven of Infinite Light (Apramāna-ābha), 3. Heaven of Supreme Light (Ābhāsvara)

The Third Dhyana, which contains, 1. Heaven of Lesser Purity (Parīttaśubha), 2. Heaven of Infinite Purity (Apramānaśubha), 3. Heaven of Universal Purity (Śubhakrtsna)

The Fourth Dhyana, which contains, 1. Cloudless Heaven (Anabhraka), 2. Merit-producing Heaven (Punyaprasava)
3. Heaven of Greater Fruits (Brhatphala), 4. Heaven Free of Trouble (Abrha), 5. Heaven without Affliction (Atapa)
6. Heaven of Excellent Viewing (Sudrśa), 7. Heaven of Excellent Observation (Sudarśana), 8. Highest Heaven (Akanistha)

[28] In the **World of Non-form (arupyadhatu)** there are four heavenly realms:
Abode of Boundless Space (ākāśa-ānantya-āyatana)
Abode of Boundless Consciousness (vijnāna-ānantya-āyatana)

In short, there are many experiences that sentient beings can enjoy, from sexual instincts, hate, anger, greed, jealousy, pride, pleasurable distractions, to various absorptions and spiritual pleasures. These can generate even in this life, the states of mind corresponding to the various planes of existence which, after the karmic effect of being born here is exhausted, they will lead to an actual rebirth in a specific plane of existence.

Of course, these emotions are often found in various combinations inside our conscience, and we are a mixture of hate, pride, sexual desire, avarice, greed, etc, but sometimes our lives can become dominated by a specific emotion, which can thus weigh heavier than the rest, and determine our future rebirth. Hitler or Stalin, for example, are the perfect example of beings who were dominated by hate and anger which resulted in mass murder. Thus, even if they lived more than fifty years in human form and human dimension, their minds already resembled those of the hell dwellers, and I am sure that after their physical death and departure from this realm, their mental continuum was reborn in one of the hells.

As I previously said, because we are the creators of our emotions, we are too, the creators of the dimensions and realms which correspond to them. Just like in one night we dream of walking in a beautiful garden, because we did some good deeds and had compassionate thoughts toward others during the day, we can also be reborn in a gods realm after a life in which we kept the negative emotions in some kind of balance, but we still could not reach freedom from any of them. Or as in a nightmare in which we are hunted down by fierce animals and monsters, after we were immersed in thoughts of hate and murder for a day or a week, we can also be reborn in various hells, after a life filled with constant killing and angry behavior. As we have in us the potential and the seed of every dimension and realm, we alone are responsible for our present and future destiny. No so called "creator-god" has any role in this and no one can be blamed, except us. According to Shakyamuni Buddha, to

Abode of Nothingness (ākincanya-āyatana)
Abode of Neither Thought nor Non-thought (naiva-samjnā-na-asamjnā-āyatana)

accept the existence of a creator god would undermine the idea of moral responsibility, as it would mean that the six negative emotions (or the potentiality of having such emotions), which are the cause for the transmigration of unenlightened beings, were also created by him, and so he can be blamed for not making his creatures right:

"He who has eyes can see the sickening sight;
Why does not Brahma [equivalent to creator god idea] set his creatures right?

If his [Brahma] wide power no limit can restrain [if he is omnipresent and omnipotent],
Why is his hand so rarely spread to bless?
Why are all his creatures condemned to pain?
Why does he not to all give happiness?
Why do fraud, lies, and ignorance prevail [if he is omni-benevolent]?
Why triumphs falsehood — truth and justice fail?
I count your Brahma one the unjust among
Who made a world in which to shelter wrong."[29]

Shakyamuni Buddha also said:

"If a creator god (Isvara) were to determine the life of all beings, including their happiness and misery, virtue and vice, then man is carrying out the commandments of that god. Therefore, it would be god who would be smeared by their actions."

"If there exists some lord all-powerful to fulfill
In every creature bliss or woe, and action good or ill,
That lord is stained with sin.
The human being does but works his will".[30]

Thus, the realms themselves, the worlds and universes appear due to causes and conditions, which are, mainly, our own karma, just like the beautiful dreams or nightmares appear due to our own thoughts and deeds. Although the entire Samsara with its myriad of worlds,

---

[29] *Bhuridatta Jataka,* No. 453
[30] *Mahabodhi Jataka,* No. 528

and filled with the six types of beings, appears to be distinct and solid, it is in fact dreamy and insubstantial.

If a dream is an individual manifestation of karmic traces, in the case of the realms of existence the karmic traces are collective. Because of the collective karma, the beings in each realm share similar experiences in a consensual world. Collective karma creates bodies, senses, and mental capacities that allow individuals to participate in shared potentials and categories of experience, while making other kinds of experience impossible. This is why, for example, some animals can hear sounds that humans cannot, while humans experience language in ways animals cannot[31]. The same can be said for every category of beings from various dimensions of existence and worlds. There is a famous Buddhist explanation which sheds light upon this matter, according to which the same river appear as fire for the hell dwellers, as a hallucination which quickly disappear when approached by a hungry ghost, as a river of water for human beings and as a river of ambrosia for the gods. This clearly shows that unenlightened beings actually see what their karma makes them see, and live in places where their karma leads them to live - places which are the manifestation of karmic traces themselves. So, if the same river looks different for different kinds of beings, some of them drinking from it, while others being burned by it, then which is the true nature of the river? Does it really exist as an independent and distinct material part of the world, or is just an element of the Samsaric dream? If the first would be true, then why the Buddhas, who are the only Awakened Ones, are not hurt nor influenced by it? Thus, we can now see that although it appears substantially and solid for unenlightened beings attached to forms, it is in fact dreamlike and insubstantial for those who see and live in the True Reality or Buddhahood. As Bodhisattva Nagarjuna explained:

"There is no reality in a dream but nevertheless we believe in the reality of the things seen in a dream. After waking up [becoming Buddhas], we recognize the falsity of the dream and we smile at ourselves. In the same way, the person deep in the sleep of the fetters

---

[31] *The Tibetan Yogas of Dream and Sleep*, by Tenzin Wangyal Rinpoche, Snow Lion, Boston & London, 1998, p. 34.

(samyojananidra) clings (abhiniviśate) to the things that do not exist; but when he has found the Path, at the moment of Enlightenment, he understands that there is no reality and laughs at himself. This is why it is said: like in a dream.

Moreover, by the power of sleep (nidrābala), the dreamer sees something there where there is nothing. In the same way, by the power of the sleep of ignorance (avidyānidrā), a person believes in the existence of all kinds of things that do not exist, e.g., 'me' and 'mine' (ātmātmīya), male and female, etc.

Moreover, in a dream, we enjoy ourselves although there is nothing enjoyable there; we are irritated although there is nothing irritating there; we are frightened although there is nothing to be afraid of there. In the same way, beings of the threefold world (traidhātukasattva), in the sleep of ignorance, are irritated although there is nothing irritating, enjoy themselves although there is nothing enjoyable, and frightened although there is nothing to be afraid of."[32]

Unenlightened beings are physically and mentally limited by their karma; they are born, they live, die and are reborn again in worlds determined by their karma. They cannot go further than the limitations imposed by their karma, and so they cannot see nor understand that which is beyond their karma. But the Buddhas[33], who

---

32 Nagarjuna, *Mahaprajñaparamitopadesa*, Chapter XI
[33] There are 10 epithets of the Buddha who show their attainment of Enlightenment:
   1.   Tathagata (lit., „the one coming from Thusness"/ „thus-come" or „thus-gone" – the term is construed as one who has come from, or gone to, Thusness or ultimate reality)
   2.   Arhat (lit., „one worthy of offerings")
   3.   Perfectly Enlightened One
   4.   One Possesed of Perfect Knowledge and Practice
   5.   Well-gone
   6.   One Having Good Knowledge of the World
   7.   Unsurpassed One
   8.   Tamer of People
   9.   Teacher of devas (gods) and humans
  10. World Honored One

are totally free from the bondage of karma, can move freely[34] in the Samsaric worlds and universes - the collective dreams of unenlightened beings. The Buddhas are not creators of the Samsaric world, just like one person cannot create the dream of another, but teachers and saviors, or better said, **Awakeners of others**. Through various means, that is, various Dharma methods, they try to awake sleeping beings from the Samsaric dream.

Thus, as Buddhists, we cannot say that a creator god made the universe, because that would deny the law of karma, according to which one reaps what one saw – one is reborn in the worlds and dimensions one deserves, together with the beings one deserves to be there (is karmically linked to). As we have seen, we cannot logically accept, in the same time, the law of karma and the existence of a creator god, as the two mutually exclude one another.

*

Instead of a creator god, **the collective karma of a multitude number of beings is the primary cause and first impulse for the appearance of a new universe. This karma contains all the potentiality of that specific universe, including its general laws of physics**. Thus, once it comes into existence from collective karmic causes, then all the laws of physics will follow. These will be responsible, for example, with what actually happens with the planets, changing of seasons, and so on. It is very important to understand that if the collective karma is the primary cause for the formation/apparition of a new universe, not all the things which happen next in that universe is due to karma. For example, when a leaf falls from a tree, or when a rock falls from a mountain, it is not the karma of the leaf or the rock to fall, but the simple law of

---

[34] There are six general powers (supernatural abilities/faculties) attributed to the Buddhas: 1) the ability to go anywhere at will, 2) the ability to see things at any distance, 4)the ability to hear sounds at any distance, 5)the ability to see into the minds of others, 6) the ability to recollect one's own previous lives and those of others, and 7) the ability to eliminate all evil passions

gravitation. If we happen to walk in the mountain when a rock falls, and we are hit in the head, then that is karma, but no matter we are there or not, rocks and leaves will fall, and planets will revolve around the sun, etc. Thus, once a universe appeared, not everything which happens in it can be called karma. However, I repeat, **the impulse and the primal cause which brought that universe into existence is the collective karma of the beings that have the causes for rebirth in such physical conditions.**

Various universes may have different laws of physics, because their formation was due to a different karma with different potentialities, so once they are formed, they can developed into different ways than our own universe. Because of that, what we call human beings here, may look totally different in another universe, although the basic emotions and karma which generate rebirth into human dimension is the same.

Neither the law of karma, nor the various physical characteristics that appear in a specific universe, are created by a supreme god. Just like when you spit in the air, it will fall in your face or when you piss against the wind, you will get wet, when you do an evil deed, you will automatically experience (in the same life or one of the next) the same suffering you inflicted on others. These things happen without the necessity that a supreme god gives a command and say, "from now on, if you spit in the air, it will fall on your face, or if you piss against the wind, you will get wet". So, the law of karma, just like the law of gravity, has no creator, as both exist by themselves.

Because individuals and various smaller or larger groups of beings make certain choices, and plant certain seeds, they reap various results, which bring them for rebirth in different universes and realms – which are themselves the effect of those beings collective karma. Thus, **the difference among unenlightened beings and the worlds and dimensions in which they live do not have the origin in the will of a creator god, nor they appear from chance, but are the material imprint of individual karma and collective karma.** This is a very important teaching which clearly separates Buddhism from the monotheistic religions. In short, the karma versus the will of a god are the two main explanations of the world and the beings living in it that you can chose from, and which defines you as a Buddhist disciple or an externalist (non-Buddhist).

*

According to the Buddhist teaching, there are an infinite number of world systems where rebirth[35] takes place. These were classified into three categories:

1. **one small universe**, which is traditionally called "a small one thousand-world". It consists of one thousand worlds. Each single world (sometimes called "a Sumeru-world") contains the various realms/dimensions of hells, hungry ghosts, animals, humans, asuras and gods.

2. **one middle universe**, which is traditionally called "a medium one thousand-world". It consists of one thousand small universes (or "a thousand small thousand-worlds").

3. **one large universe**, which is traditionally called, "a great one thousand-world". It consists of one thousand middle universes (or a thousand medium thousand-worlds).

These various worlds pass through and endless cycle of formation, existence, destruction, and annihilation after which they are again formed, come to existence, are destroyed, annihilated, and so on. The four periods of cyclic changes are called "kalpas":

1. Period (kalpa) of Formation or generation (vivartakalpa)

2. Period (kalpa) of Duration or existence (vivarta-siddha kalpa)

3. Period (kalpa) of Destruction (samvarta kalpa)

4. Period (kalpa) of Annihilation (samvarta-diddha kalpa)

---

35 There are four modes of birth: (1) birth from womb, like human beings, some animals and devas (gods) inhabiting the earth, (2) birth from the egg, like birds and fishes, (3) from moisture, like some insects and worms, and (4) spontaneous birth, such as gods, pretas (hungry spirits) and hell-dwellers. I'll describe in detail, in the following pages, the characteristics of these beings.

Each of these periods lasts 20 medium or intermediate kalpas[36] (antara kalpa). Four periods of 20 medium kalpas each, is 80 medium kalpas. 80 medium kalpas is one great kalpa (mahakalpa). So, **one cosmic cycle composed of the four periods above is called one great kalpa**.

One Buddha may assume responsibility for the spiritual care of one large universe ("a great one thousand-world"), which then becomes that Buddha's field of action, or "Buddha-field" (Buddhakshetra in Skt). This is also called a "Buddha-land". The one large universe in which we ourselves live together with many kinds of visible, invisible and non-human beings, is called "Saha". The sutras say that an infinite number of such large universes, or Buddha-lands, exist in the ten directions. As they are inhabited by beings in various stages of spiritual development, it should not be confounded with the Pure Land (Sukhavati), which is an Enlightened realm (outside of Samsara) manifested by Amida Buddha.

Of course, not all the worlds and universes appear or disappear at the same time. When one universe is destroyed, another one appears while myriads of other universes are in the duration period. Also, the mind-stream of beings transmigrates through these universes and planes of existence in all the four kalpas, and the period of destruction or annihilation does not destroy them. Thus, even if the bodies they receive according to their karma are destroyed, they are reborn elsewhere, in another realm of the same universe or even another universe.

---

36 A single small kalpa is so long that it can only be described metaphorically. According to one metaphor, it is even longer than the period of time required of a person to empty a walled city full of poppy seeds, one cubic yojana (a unit equivalent to the distance which a royal army can march in a day) in size, by removing one seed every hundred years. According to another metaphor it is the length of time required for a rock, 40 cubic ri in size, to be worn away as a celestial maiden passes over the rock once every three years touching it lightly with its feather robe.
Some scholars say that one kalpa is the equivalent of 1,000 yugas, or 4,320,000,000 years.

It is in the nature of every composed thing, including planets, worlds and universes to appear, grow, decay and dissolve themselves. When the collective karma which brought them into existence is exhausted, they are to appear again when another collective karma manifest itself.

Two questions on Buddha nature and Samsara

Question 1: "Where did the Buddha nature within us originally come from?"

Question 2: "When did the process of self-delusion or suffering start the first time and why?"

First of all, no matter how much a Buddha would explain to us the nature of the universe, Buddha-nature, Nirvana, etc., as long as we are unenlightened beings with limited mental/spiritual capacities, we cannot truly understand it. So, the Buddha only offered us some hints or clues (like those I presented above), but He could not possibly offer to us everything we want to know, and not because He did not know, but because we do not have the right organ or spiritual maturity for knowing more. Just imagine how can you explain a physical theory to a newborn baby – it is not because you do not know it, but because the baby cannot really understand you at the level he is now. Our brain or what we call "mind" cannot really process the wisdom of a Buddha who naturally knows everything. Thus, only when we ourselves attain Buddhahood we can understand everything about Buddha nature and Samsara, and all our questions will be answered or better said, we'll have no question to ask because then we will naturally know everything, and where there is no ignorance, there are no questions .

This is why the Buddha insisted that here and now we should be concentrated on following the Path and reach Nirvana, as a person wounded by a poisoned arrow will first pull the arrow out instead of dealing with theories like, "to which bird did the feathers of the arrow belonged to", or "what type of wood was used when making that arrow", and so on.

The unenlightened human mind is limited and dualist, so it has the tendency to think in terms of beginning and end. But this, "beginning and end" are just "mind categories", nothing more. Sometimes they are useful tools, especially in dealing with everyday life, but when we wish to use them to understand Nirvana or Buddha nature, they are not so useful anymore, and rather they can become obstacles. Thus, because we cannot overcome duality, it is impossible for us to conceive that which is beyond beginning and end. The truth is that the mind wishes very much to be a beginning, because this gives her a sense of security, stability, and some kind of false understanding which is in fact, an intellectual concept, not true knowing. Because our mind functions in terms of "beginning and end", it might appear safe for it to accept the idea of a creator-god. Indeed, the human mind feels safer if it wraps up the world in concepts which seem familiar to it. So, for many people, the matter is not if "there is or there is not a creator god", but rather, "it must be a creator", and so they will actually do everything to cling to the idea of a creator-god.

Coming back to the Buddha-nature or Nirvana, sometimes the Buddha used positive and negative descriptions of it, so as to make us yearn for freedom, or wish to become Buddhas ourselves, or to give us a starting point, but He also pointed out that: *"Nirvana is beyond concepts"*. This is to show us that we cannot apply any mind category to it. So, without entering into details which are impossible to comprehend with our limited minds, **Nirvana or Buddha nature is the state of true freedom, while Samsara is the state of bondage or slavery**. You are free or you are not free, or in other words, you are either a Buddha or an unenlightened being. No god created the state of samsaric slavery and its myriad of realms (as I explained in the last subchapter), just as no god created the state of true freedom. **Being uncreated, the state of Nirvana or Buddha nature has no beginning and no end, so we cannot say that it came from here or there.** Only about the karmic existences we can say they are created over and over again by unenlightened beings who are self-illusioned. But as to "when this process of self-delusion or suffering started in the first place and why" - this is a question asked in the dream by a sleeping (unenlightened) person using dreaming categories, with a mind which does not know freedom and awakening, and which will be answered after Awakening (Buddhahood) or better, the questions will naturally disappear after Awakening.

Once we attain true freedom or Awakening from the Samsaric dream (Buddha means the "Awakened One"), there is no more

42

Samsara for us. This is similar with the every morning situation when we awake from a dream and we realize that the dream was not real, while **the state of awakening, or Buddha-nature, was always there.** This means that the dream was created by us and our own emotions, while the state of awakening (Buddhahood/Nirvana) is uncreated. **That which is always there, uncreated and unchanged is this Reality-when-awake or the Buddha-nature.**

Those who believe in a creator god cannot have true faith in Amida Buddha

In the previous sub-chapters I explained and counteracted the eternalist view of a supreme creator god, and I will do the same with the false views on Amida Buddha and His Pure Land in the second part of this book. But before I finish the first part, I wish to present to you my answer to a very important question raised by a Dharma friend in relation to this topic.

Question[37]:
"A lot of folks who end up in Shin Buddhism here in the West have a lot of vestigial concepts from our Abrahamic background - whether or not they were ever "believers" themselves. And they carry those vestigial ideas with them when they start in as Buddhists. Some don't do that of course - particularly the ones who are given to serious study, and really consider it important to know what Shakyamuni actually taught. But as you know from your time in both the Zen and Shin Sanghas, such study is often not the primary focus - or even as great a focus as it is in the Theravada and Tibetan Buddhist Sangha groups. [...]

So, in your opinion, based on your own reading and contemplating, is it possible for an ignorant, yet well meaning person to come to settled shinjin if he (or she) has never actually studied the subject[38], and has some mixed up ideas about eternalism stuck in his mind stream? Or is the presence of such thoughts a necessary karmic obstacle that must directly be addressed and removed before the person can receive Amida's gift of shinjin?"

Answer:

---

[37] This question was sent to me by Paul Roberts and the entire discussion can be read on the True ShinBuddhism yahoo group, at
https://groups.yahoo.com/neo/groups/true_shin_buddhism/conversations/messages/7005
[38] The subject of eternalism as the existence of a supreme creator god who is eternally abiding.

I think it depends on how important the baggage of eternalist ideas is for them or how much weight it has in their mind-stream.

Most of the people in the world today, and especially those born in a Judeo-Christian background, have a basic information about the idea of a creator god, but **I make a distinction in the way they react to it, especially if they call themselves Jodo Shinshu followers**. Some don't care too much about it – if this creator-god exists or not – because they do not find it important, and so they focus single-mindedly on Amida Buddha, while others do care about it and think it is important, thus giving it some important space in their minds. Both categories of people may claim they entrust in Amida, but I doubt that those in the second category have a genuine faith.

If, for the first category the "creator god" is just an information which they prefer not to deal with it or don't care about it, for the second category it is an actual presence which clearly has some conscious or unconscious consequences on them. I think that for people in the second category Amida is automatically thought and felt in relation with this creator-god, and according to my experience, most of them even think about Amida in terms of a superior creature or a person who is somehow lower than god. **But no matter how they place Amida in relation with this creator-god, their clinging to the god idea is the key to understand them.** This clinging is, into my opinion, a hindrance to true shinjin, which is not the case for the first category.

People in the first category, after hearing a Buddhist explanation they can easily let go to the idea of a creator god, even if until then they did not know they should actually let it go, but those in the second category will put up a fight and will try to defend it.

Of course, we can never know exactly what happens inside one's heart and only Amida knows if one really has shinjin or not, but we can also say that people are like trees, so they can be known by their fruits or in our case, **by their reactions**. Just like someone who denies the existence of Amida Buddha cannot possibly have genuine faith in Him, one who tenaciously clings to and defends the idea of a creator god, cannot possibly entrust to Amida Buddha as a supreme Savior. Also, as I previously said, one who is mentally and spiritualy

45

attached to the idea of a creator god will, consciously or unconsciusly, relate Amida Buddha to this god-creator, and he may also think that Amida is a creature himself – a creation of this god....

It is not by chance that we have an explanation by Shakyamuni, made in human terms, of who a Buddha is, who Amida is, and what is His Pure Land. Also – and this is extremely important – in the Primal Vow we are told to entrust to/have faith in Amida Buddha – which means ONLY in Amida Buddha. **To have faith in Amida Buddha means to accept that He is the supreme and unique Savior, but when we cling to the idea of a creator god, this is also an expression of faith which, in this case, is directed toward that god.** To accept the existence of a creator god, of Amida Buddha or any divine figure from any religion is not a scientific fact, but a matter of faith. So, if upon hearing Shakyamuni's teaching about the non-existence of a creator-god, some react aggresively and try to resist it, or even deny it, this is a hint that they actually have faith in that creator god. **Their very resistence is an expression of their wrong faith.**

Those who claim to have received shinjin (faith in Amida), but cling to the idea of a creator-god, actually have faith in the creator god, and a false or unsettled faith in Amida. This is my opinion, which comes not only from my contemplation on this matter or my readings, but from my experience as a priest and my meeting face to face with such people.

You asked me, "what is the minimum necessary understanding of Buddha Dharma that a person MUST have in order to receive Amida's gift?"

I cannot make a complete list and cannot relate to every particular situation and persons, but I can say that one should be helped to have a minimum Dharmic vision of the world, so he must understand in simple terms what is karma (karma and the idea of a creator god cannot actually coexist, as I explained in my previous subchapters on this topic), that rebirth is a true phenomenon filled with constant insatisfaction, and that true Freedom (Buddhas can be explained as truly Free Ones, having perfect Compassion) from these repeated births and deaths is something he should wish for ..... and for this freedom to come quickly and certainly, one needs to accept Amida's helping hand, as the only true Savior.

Even an illiterate person can have such a minimum understanding of karma, rebirth (which can be explained in terms of life after death in various forms), and of Amida Buddha as a supreme Free One who manifested a perfect world/realm where we can aspire to go after death and become Free Persons (Buddhas) ourselves, then come back to save those we love.

We can ask ourselves – if we do not consider Shakyamuni to be the supreme all-knowing Teacher in the universe (Teacher of all sentient beings, including gods and men), if we think that the Buddha can be right in some matters and wrong in others, like in His denial of the existence of a supreme creator god, then how can we listen to Him with an open mind and heart and accept His teaching on Amida Buddha from the *Larger Sutra*?

If Shakyamuni was wrong in only one thing, then how can we know He wasn't wrong when He taught about Amida and His Pure Land? We must remember that Shakyamuni urged us to accept His teaching on Amida Buddha in faith, and that it is the teaching most hardly to be accepted in faith, so how can we do this, if we do not consider Shakyamuni to be infallible in His wisdom?

Truly, the entire Dharma of Shakyamuni Buddha must be 100% true or is not true at all.

Unenlightened people (non-Buddhas) who call themselves disciples of the Buddha, cannot pick and chose what they like and discard what they don't like from the Buddha's teaching. All Buddhist doctrines are inter-related, and if one adds an alien element, like the so called, "creator god", then the whole Buddhist system is unrecognizable. Karma and the teaching on Buddha and Buddha-nature cannot co-exist with that of a supreme and eternal creator god. Thus, before we entrust to Amida Buddha and aspire to be born in His Pure Land, we must be true disciples of Shakyamuni Buddha and fully accept His teachings and explanations on Samsara.

CHAPTER II
THE TRUE TEACHING ON AMIDA
BUDDHA AND HIS PURE LAND

If Amida's Primal Vow is true...

Shinran Shonin said:

"If Amida's Primal Vow is true, Shakyamuni's teaching cannot be false. If the Buddha's teaching is true, Shan-tao's commentaries cannot be false. If Shan-tao's commentaries are true can Honen's words be lies? If Honen's words are true, then surely what I say cannot be empty."[39]

The Primal Vow is true. This is the basis of our faith and of the entire Amida Dharma which was taught by Shakyamuni and the succeeding Masters. Everything starts with this – the Primal Vow is true. If we accept that the Primal Vow is true and we rely on it without any doubt, then we are saved; if not, this life in human form is wasted:

"if in this lifetime still you are entangled in a net of doubt, then unavoidably you must pass once more in the stream of birth-and-death through myriads of kalpas".[40]

In the Primal Vow we find everything we need, and what Amida and Shakyamuni want us to do. We can say that the whole Buddhism is reduced for us, to the Primal Vow. Of course, Shakyamuni taught many things during His lifetime, but nothing is more important to us than those precious moments when He told the story of Amida Buddha and his Primal Vow. As Shinran said:

*"Among all teachings the Great Sage preached in his lifetime, none surpasses this ocean
of virtues [the Primal Vow]."*[41]

---

[39] *Tannisho,* chapter 2 - *The Collected Works of Shinran*, Shin Buddhism
Translation Series, Jodo Shinshu Hongwanji-ha, Kyoto, 1997, p.662
[40] *Kyogyoshinsho*, chapter I, *The Collected Works of Shinran*, Shin Buddhism
Translation Series, Jodo Shinshu Hongwanji-ha, Kyoto, 1997, p.4
[41] *Idem,* p.3

For Shinran and for us *"the universal Vow difficult to fathom is indeed a great vessel bearing us across the ocean difficult to cross"*. It is *"the true teaching easy to practice for small, foolish beings; the straight way easy to traverse for the dull and ignorant"*.

In the Primal Vow Amida Buddha made the following promise:

"If, when I attain Buddhahood, sentient beings in the lands of the ten quarters who sincerely and joyfully entrust themselves to me, desire to be born in my land, and call my Name, even ten times, should not be born there, may I not attain perfect Enlightenment."

Those who have faith in Him, say His Name and wish to be born in His Pure Land, will go there. It is as simple as that. Clearly, as Shinran said above, it is something that even the "dull and ignorant" can follow. No special practice, no high virtues or spiritual capacities, no this or that meditation technique, no retire into a monastery, no nothing but a simple faith, saying of His Name (faith and saying of the Name are the same) and wish to be reborn in His Pure Land after death.

The masters of our school always insisted that we must be in accord with the Primal Vow. To be in accord with the Primal Vow means that we accept it as being true and effective in saving us, that we say the Name in faith and wish to be born in Amida's Land. To accept that the Primal Vow is true and effective also means that the elements of this Vow are true and real. Which are these elements? They are Amida Buddha and His Pure Land. Only in relation with this Buddha and His Pure Land there is a faith, a saying of the Name and a wish to be born. Faith in whom? It is faith in Amida. Saying the Name of whom? Saying the Name of Amida. Wishing to be born in whose land? Wishing to be born in Amida's Land.

If we have faith in someone, then it means we are sure beyond any doubt that he is reliable and that he will keep his promise. Now I will say something which might sound too simple and obvious to be mentioned, but to believe in someone's promise means that we accept his existence, too. Promises can be made by living persons, in our case by a living, existing Amida Buddha, not by material objects or fictional characters. If you read Harry Potter or a book about Santa Claus, or even Hamlet by Shakespeare, you cannot actually believe that these characters are real. You know they are part of a fiction and whatever they say in their specific novel, you will never think they are actually promising something to you personally. Why am I saying this and make this silly comparison? It is because some nowadays deluded scholars and false teachers in our international sangha are trying very hard to convince people that Amida Buddha is just another fictional character like Hamlet[42], and not a real Enlightened Person. They also try to present the other element of the Primal Vow – the Pure Land – as being non-existent or something to be attained here and now, in this very existence, and not a place where we should desire to be reborn after death, as the Primal Vow urges us to do.

The situation is very complicated and it would take many pages and even many books to describe in detail the various aspects of these wrong views and heresies, including their so called arguments, or the reason why their authors are acting like that. However, in this book I intend to offer you not just another theory or personal opinion, but the only view that matters – the true teaching about Amida Buddha and his Pure Land, as it was taught by Shakyamuni and the Masters of our tradition.

So, coming back to our line of arguments, only if we accept the actual existence of Amida Buddha in Form and Name and of His Pure Land, we can have a genuine faith in Him, say His Name and wish to be born there. Because Amida Buddha and His Pure Land are true and real, His Primal Vow, in which he urges us to entrust to Him, say His Name and wish to go there, is itself true and real. We are not speaking here about an empty promise made by an unenlightened person, or by a fictional character in a fantasy book, but about the promise of a real Buddha, the fully Enlightened One called Amida.

---

[42] Dr Nobuo Haneda actually said *"Amida is 'a fictional character' like Hamlet or Faust"* in his article *What Is Amida Buddha?*, published on
http://www.livingdharma.org/Living.Dharma.Articles/WhatIsAmida-Haneda.html

Because He exists and He is a Buddha, then it means He is reliable and we can let him carry us to His Pure Land.

Next, where do we hear about Amida Buddha, His Land and his Primal Vow? We hear about them in the teaching of Shakyamuni, the historical Buddha who appeared in our world more than 2500 years ago. This is another reason to entrust our karmic destiny to Amida – because Shakyamuni is the witness and the one who told Amida's story to us:

"If Amida's Primal Vow is true, Shakyamuni's teaching cannot be false"

Master Seikaku made a very simple statement about accepting the Primal Vow in faith on the basis that Shakyamuni himself told us about it and the One who made this Vow:

"Suppose that a man whom one deeply trusts and of whom one has no cause for suspicion whatever, tells you about a place which he knows well at firsthand, saying that there is a mountain here, a river there. You believe deeply what he says, and after you have accepted these words, you meet other people who say it is all false. There is no mountain and no river.

Nevertheless, since what you heard was said by a person whom you cannot think would speak a mere fabrication, a hundred thousand people might tell you differently but you would not accept it. Rather, you deeply trust what you heard first. This is called trust. Now, believing in what Sakyamuni taught, entrusting yourself to Amida's Vow, and being without any doubt should be like this."43

Also the Masters of our tradition who followed Shakyamuni, including Shan-tao, Honen and Shinran[44] accepted and transmitted to us the truth of the Primal Vow:

---

[43] *Essentials of Faith Alone* by Master Seikaku.
[44] Also Nagarjuna, Vasubandhu, T'an-luan, Tao-ch'o, Genshin, Rennyo Shonin.

"If the Buddha's teaching is true, Shan-tao's commentaries cannot be false. If Shan-tao's commentaries are true, can Honen's words be lies? If Honen's words are true, then surely what I say cannot be empty".

Even if they sometimes used different methods, they all taught that Amida and His Pure Land exist and that we should have faith and desire to go there.

These being said, I now move to the next phase of this book, in which I try to explain in more detail who is Amida Buddha and the Pure Land. In my explanations I will rely of course, not on my own opinions, but on the teaching of Shakyamuni and the succeeding Masters. Only by submitting my mind and heart to their teaching, and thus to the Primal Vow, the words I use cannot be empty and false.

The story of Amida Buddha as told by Shakyamuni Buddha

Because we are unenlightened, we cannot fully comprehend with our limited minds everything that is related with Amida Buddha and His Pure Land. But because we were given a teaching and guidance on how to look at them and how to accept them, I think it is good if we know these instructions, so that we can never be misguided by others.

Shakyamuni Buddha's main teaching about Amida Buddha can be found in the Three Pure Land Sutras[45], among which the *Larger Sutra* is the most important. In fact, Shinran thought that teaching this sutra was the main reason for Shakyamuni's appearance on earth[46]. He was also convinced that the *Larger Sutra* is the true teaching of the Buddha Dharma, while all other methods and teachings Shakyamuni preached during His lifetime, are provisory. Here are just a few important passages from his *Kyogyoshinsho* that support this vision:

"To reveal the true teaching: It is the Larger Sutra of the Buddha of Immeasurable Life. The central purport of this sutra is that Amida, by establishing the incomparable Vows, has opened wide the Dharma

---

[45] The Three Pure Land sutras are:
1) *Sutra on the Buddha of Infinite Life* (Larger *Sukhavativyuha Sutra* in Skt./*Bussetsu Muryōju Kyo* in Jpn.); it is often called *Larger Sutra*. This sutra was translated into Chinese during the Ts'ao-Wei dynasty (252 C.E.), by Tripitaka Master Samghavarman (Kosogai in Jpn.).
2) *Sutra on Visualisation of the Buddha of Infinite Life* (*Amitayurdhyana Sutra* in Skt./*Bussetsu Kanmuryoju Kyo* in Jpn.); it is often called *Contemplation Sutra*. This sutra was translated into Chinese during the Liu-Sung dynasty (424-442 C.E.) by the Tripitaka Master Kalayasas (Kyoryoyasha).
3) *Sutra on the Amitayus Buddha* (Smaller *Sukhavativyuha Sutra* in Skt./*Bussetsu Amida Kyo* in Jpn.); it is often called *Smaller Sutra*. This sutra was translated into Chinese during the Yao-Ch'in dynasty (402 C.E.), by the Tripitaka Master Kumarajiva (Kumaraju in Jpn).
[46] See the chapter „The reason for Shakyamuni's appearance in this world" from my book, *Jodo Shinshu Buddhist Teachings*, Dharma Lion Publications, Craiova, 2011, p32

54

storehouse, and full of compassion for small, foolish beings, selects and bestows the treasure of virtues. [The sutra further reveals that] Shakyamuni appeared in this world and expounded the teachings of the way to Enlightenment, seeking to save the multitudes of living beings by blessing them with this benefit that is true and real[47]. Thus, to teach the Tathagata's Primal Vow is the true intent of this sutra; the Name of the Buddha is its essence"[48].

"[...] the Larger Sutra reveals the true teaching. It is indeed the right exposition for which the Tathagata appeared in the world, the wondrous scripture rare and most excellent, the conclusive and ultimate exposition of the One Vehicle[49], the precious words disclosing perfect, instantaneous fulfillment, the sincere words praised by all the Buddhas throughout the ten quarters, the true teaching in consummate readiness for the beings of this day. Let this be known"[50].

He also said in his *Hymn of True Faith and the Nembutsu (Shoshinge)*:

"*The reason for the Buddha's appearance in the world
Is, above all, to expound the Primal Vow of Amida, wide and deep as the ocean.
All beings in the evil age of the five defilements
Should believe in the truth of the Buddha's words.*[51] "

---

[47] *„The benefit that is true and real"* is the infinite merit and virtue of Amida embodied in His Name. To say His Name in faith, desiring to be born in His Land, is what the Primal Vow urges us to do.

[48] *The Collected Works of Shinran*, Shin Buddhism Translation Series, Jodo Shinshu Hongwanji-ha, Kyoto, 1997, p.7

[49] „One vehicle" („Ichijo" in Jpn or „Ekayana" in Skrt) is the complete and supreme Dharma of the Buddha which provides the method of attaining Buddhahood quickly.

[50] *The Collected Works of Shinran*, Shin Buddhism Translation Series, Jodo Shinshu Hongwanji-ha, Kyoto, 1997, p.10

[51] *The Way of Nembutsu-Faith: A Commentary on the Shoshinge*, by Hisao Inagaki, Nagata Bunshodo, Kyoto, 1996, pp. 163-183. The same translation can be found at http://horai.eu/shoshinge-eng.htm

So, for us, disciples of Shakyamuni and Shinran, this sutra[52] is supreme and all the teachings and events related in it are to be

---

[52] There are some who deny the authenticity of the Mahayana sutras in general, and of the three Pure Land sutras, in particular, saying that because they appeared later in written form, they are in fact, the creation of some monks. Many Theravadins share the same opinion on this matter and claim that their Pali canon is the only authentic set of sutras. However, **common sense dictates that the time when a Buddhist sutra was put into written form was not automatically the time of its creation.** During Shakyamuni Buddha's life and later, upon His physical death, His discourses (sutras) were transmitted orally and sometimes by His closest disciples through special states of mind called Samadhi for hundreds of years before they were put into written form. The Pali Canon was, in fact, preserved in the artificial language of Pali (which neither the Buddha nor anyone else ever spoke) while the Mahayana sutras were initially preserved in Sanskrit (a language which Shakyamuni, a highly educated person, may have spoken). Some make the claim that the Pali Canon of the Theravada school is the oldest and thus the most reliable collection of sutras. **Positing that all the discourses or sutras originated from Shakyamuni, then the fact that some were put into written form earlier than the others is not proof of their exclusive authenticity or superior content.** The Mahayana and Pure Land sutras did exist and were transmitted in the same timeframe with the sutras of the Pali Canon.

Each group of Buddhist disciples put into written form their own basket (pitaka) of recognized sutras, some earlier and some later. But no one can prove by documentary evidence that his school's basket of sutras were actually preached by Shakyamuni while the others' were not. By the same token, **no one can prove** that Shakyamuni did not impart some sutras only to a group of special disciples which were open and more prepared to receive them than others and who, in turn, transmitted such sutras to their own chosen disciples in an uninterrupted succession, until one day they decided it was time to give them a written form. **No one can check and investigate the Buddha's mind or the minds of His closest disciples and their actions by means of documentary evidence.** If we read about the Buddhist councils who compiled orally the discourses of the Buddha after His physical death, we see that the monks who attended such councils could all recite by heart dozens of those discourses and that all were accomplished Masters.

Also, we know from the first passages of the Sutra on the Buddha of Immeasurable Life (Larger Sutra), that among the assembly gathered on the Vulture Peak, where Shakyamuni delivered it, there were *"twelve thousand monks [...] all great sages who had already attained supernatural powers."* This aspect is extremely important because it is an indication about who were the monks who heard that sutra and later transmitted it to further generations. **They were monks who had** *"attained supernatural powers,"* **and it follows that these monks used their**

accepted as true. As Shakyamuni Himself encouraged us, we have to accept this sutra in faith:

"You should single heartedly accept in faith, uphold, and chant this sutra, and practice in accordance with its teachings"[53].

*

Now let us see what Shakyamuni told us about Amida Buddha and his Pure Land.

In section 4 of the *Larger Sutra* He first enumerates many Buddhas of the past eons of time who appeared in samsara to teach the Dharma: *"in the distant past – innumerable, incalculable and inconceivable kalpas ago..."[54].*

---

mind power to accurately transmit this sutra by Samadhi to others. Among these monks we read the names of Venerable Mahakasyapa, Venerable Sariputra, Venerable Mahamaudgalyayana and Ananda. *"All of these were Elders"*, says the sutra. But monks with supernatural powers were not the only listeners. Great transcendental Bodhisattvas like Samantabhadra, Manjusri and Maitreya, the future Buddha, were present too, and they all rejoiced at hearing the Amida Dharma, which can only mean they had faith in it and later helped in its promotion.

[53] *The Three Pure Land Sutras - A Study and Translation from Chinese* by Hisao Inagaki in collaboration with Harold Stewart, Bukkyo Dendo Kyokai and Numata Center for Buddhist Translation and Research, Kyoto, 2003, p.70

[54] *"In the distant past—innumerable, incalculable, and inconceivable kalpas ago—a Tathagata named Dipankara appeared in the world. Having taught and freed innumerable beings and led them all along the Way of enlightenment, he passed into Nirvana. Next appeared a Tathagata named Far-reaching Illumination. After him came Moonlight, and then Sandalwood Incense, King of Beautiful Mountains, Crown of Mount Sumeru, Brilliant like Mount Sumeru, Color of the Moon, Right Recollection, Free of Defilement, Nonattachment, Dragon Deva, Nocturnal Light, Peaceful and Brilliant Peak, Immovable Ground, Exquisite Beryl Flower, Golden Beryl Luster, Gold Treasury, Flaming Light, Fiery Origin, Earth Shaking, Image of the Moon, Sound of the Sun, Flower of Freedom, Glorious Light, Miraculous Power of the Ocean of Enlightenment, Water Light, Great Fragrance, Free of Dust and Defilement, Abandoning Enmity, Flame of Jewels, Beautiful Peak, Heroic Stance, Merit-possessing Wisdom, Outshining the Sun and Moon, Beryl Light of the Sun and Moon, Supreme Beryl Light, Highest Peak, Flower of Enlightenment, Brightness of the Moon, Sunlight, King of the Colors of Flowers, Moonlight on the*

Doing so, He showed to us that human history, as we know it, is only a very small fraction of the endless and inconceivable time of the universe and that the various world systems and beings living in them had existed before the appearance of this earth. So He mentioned 52 great Buddhas who appeared in samsara, taught the Dharma and entered Nirvana before the story of Amida actually happened. After these 52 Buddhas, another great Buddha named Lokesvararaja appeared, still in a distant, and impossible to explain, time and place:

"Then there appeared a Buddha named Lokesvararaja, the Tathagata, Arhat, Fully Enlightened One, Possessed of Wisdom and Practice, Well-gone One, Knower of the World, Unsurpassed One, Tamer of Beings, Teacher of Gods and Humans, and Enlightened and World-honored One".[55]

During the time and place of this Buddha, there lived a king who, after hearing His teaching, renounced the throne and became a monk (bhiksu) named, Dharmakara:

"At that time there was a king who, having heard the Buddha's exposition of the Dharma, rejoiced in his heart and awakened aspiration for highest, perfect Enlightenment. He renounced his kingdom and throne, and became a monk named Dharmakara".[56]

As the sutra tells us, this monk, Dharmakara, was already a superior person when he went to see Lokesvararaja Buddha:

Water, Dispelling the Darkness of Ignorance, Practice of Removing Hindrances, Pure Faith, Storehouse
of Good, Majestic Glory, Wisdom of the Dharma, Voice of the Phoenix, Roar of the Lion, Cry of the Dragon, and Dwelling in the World. All these Buddhas have already passed into Nirvana."
(*The Three Pure Land Sutras - A Study and Translation from Chinese* by Hisao Inagaki in collaboration with Harold Stewart, Bukkyo Dendo Kyokai and Numata Center for Buddhist Translation and Research, Kyoto, 2003, p.9)
[55] *The Three Pure Land Sutras - A Study and Translation from Chinese* by Hisao Inagaki in collaboration with Harold Stewart, Bukkyo Dendo Kyokai and Numata Center for Buddhist Translation and Research, Kyoto, 2003, p.9-10.
[56] *Idem.*, p.10.

"Having superior intelligence, courage, and wisdom, he distinguished himself in the world. He went to see Tathagata Lokesvararaja, knelt down at his feet, walked around him three times keeping him always on his right, prostrated himself on the ground, and, putting his palms together in worship, praised the Buddha".[57]

Then he informed him about the spiritual decision he took to become a Buddha himself for the sake of all sentient beings:
"I resolve to become a Buddha,
Equal in attainment to you, O Holy King of the Dharma,
To save living beings from birth and death,
And to lead them all to liberation."[58]

And in fulfilling his aspiration he mentions the creation of a special land:

"When I have become a Buddha,
My land shall be most exquisite."[59]

Where to bring sentient beings everywhere and make them perfectly happy:

"Those who come from the ten directions
Will find joy and serenity of heart;
When they reach my land,
They shall dwell in peace and happiness."[60]

To make them perfectly happy means, of course, to help them attain Nirvana, His land being in fact, a manifestation of Nirvanic bliss and freedom:

"The seat of Enlightenment will be supreme.
My land, being like Nirvana itself,

---

[57] *Ibid.*
[58] *Idem.*, p.11.
[59] *Idem.*, p.12.
[60] *Ibid.*

Will be beyond comparison."[61]

After He said the above words, He invites Lokesvararaja Buddha and all Buddhas to see into His mind and heart, and become witness to the truth of His aspiration:

"I beg you, the Buddha, to become my witness
And to vouch for the truth of my aspiration.

The World-honored Ones in the ten directions
Have unhindered wisdom;
I call upon those Revered Ones
To bear witness to my intention".[62]

However, Dharmakara needed a practice to fulfill His aspiration to become a Buddha and establish a special land/realm where to bring all beings to Nirvana, so He also asked Lokesvararaja Buddha for guidance:

"I beseech you to explain the Dharma to me fully, so that I can perform practices for the establishment of a pure Buddha land adorned with innumerable excellent qualities. So please teach me how to attain Enlightenment quickly and to remove the roots of the afflictions of birth and death of all.'"[63]

More exactly, he asked Lokesvararaja to show to Him all the Buddha-lands of the ten direction, so that He can better know what to do and how to practice to create His own Buddha-land:

"I sincerely beseech you, World Honored One, to explain in detail the practices by which Buddha Tathagatas established their pure lands. After I hear that, I wish to practice as instructed and so fulfill my aspirations."[64]

---

[61] *Ibid.*
[62] *Ibid.*
[63] *Idem.*, p.12-13.
[64] *Ibid.*

As Shakyamuni Buddha told us in the *Larger Sutra*, Lokesvararaja Buddha, *"recognized Bhiksu Dharmakara's noble and high aspirations"* and *"explained in detail the greater and lesser aspects of two hundred and ten kotis of Buddha-lands, together with the good and evil natures of heavenly and human beings living there. He revealed them all to the bhiksu just as he had requested".*[65]

Then, *"having heard the Buddha's exposition of the glorious pure lands and also having seen all of them"*, **Dharmakara *"resolved upon his supreme, unsurpassed vows".*[66]**

At this point, the sutra tells us again (for the second time)[67], that Dharmakara was not an ordinary practitioner, when He resolved to make His vows: *"his mind being serene and his aspirations free of attachment, he was unexcelled throughout the world"*[68].

As Shakyamuni told us, Dharmakara contemplated the vows he was about to make for five full kalpas and then he chose the necessary practices to fulfill them:

"For five full kalpas he contemplated the vows and then chose the pure practices for the establishment of his Buddha-land."[69]

To practice sitting meditation for even 5 hours a day is an extremely hard job for any practitioner nowadays, not to mention to sit for one day, seven days, a few months or a year, but to contemplate continuously for five full kalpas is truly beyond our capacity to understand. No wonder then that hearing about the time Dharmakara spent in contemplation, Ananda immediately asked the Buddha to specify how long was the lifespan of beings who belonged to the time and land of Lokesvararaja:

---

[65] *Ibid.*
[66] *Ibid.*
[67] First time, at the begining of the story of Dharmakara, Shakyamuni mentions, *"Having superior intelligence, courage, and wisdom, he distinguished himself in the world"*. This is important to keep in mind, for when I will explain later the doctrine of the Two Dharma Body of Amida Buddha.
[68] *The Three Pure Land Sutras - A Study and Translation from Chinese* by Hisao Inagaki in collaboration with Harold Stewart, Bukkyo Dendo Kyokai and Numata Center for Buddhist Translation and Research, Kyoto, 2003, p.13.
[69] *Ibid.*

"Ananda asked the Buddha, 'How long was the lifespan of beings in the land of Buddha Lokesvararāja?' The Buddha replied, 'The length of life of that Buddha was forty-two kalpas.'"[70]

So, after five kalpas of contemplation, Dharmakara Bodhisattva *"adopted the pure practices that had led to the establishment of the excellent lands of two hundred and ten kotis of Buddhas".*

Thus, being sure about the Vows and what practices to follow, He went to inform Lokesvararaja Buddha:

"He went to the Buddha, knelt down at his feet, walked around Him three times, joined his palms in worship, and sat down. He then said to the Buddha, 'I have adopted the pure practices for the establishment of a glorious Buddha-land.'"[71]

Having heard the Dharmakara's wonderful vows, Lokesvararaja was overjoyed and asked Him to proclaim them to the entire assembly:

"The Buddha said to him, 'You should proclaim this. Know that now is the right time. Encourage and delight the entire assembly. Hearing this, other bodhisattvas will practice this Dharma and so fulfill their innumerable great vows.'
The bhiksu replied, 'I beg you to grant me your attention. Now I will fully proclaim my vows.'"[72]

So, the entire section 7 of the *Larger Sutra* contains the list of the 48 Vows of Dharmakara. Detailed explanations of the most important among them will be made in the next chapters of this book[73], but for the moment, I wish to continue with the story told in the sutra.

---

[70] *Ibid.*

[71] *Idem.*, p.14

[72] *Ibid.*

[73] For a full of explanation of all the 48 vows, see my book, *The 48 Vows of Amida Buddha*, Dharma Lion Publications, Craiova, 2014. Free online edition can be found on Amidaji website:

Then, after listing the 48 Vows Shakyamuni described the various practices Dharmakara engaged into for *"inconceivable and innumerable kalpas"* in order to become a Buddha and manifest His Pure Land:

*"Then, Ananda, after proclaiming and establishing those universal vows in the presence of Buddha Lokesvararaja before the multitude of beings, including the eight kinds of superhuman beings, such as devas and dragon spirits, and also Mara and Brahma, Bhiksu Dharmakara was solely intent on producing a glorious and exquisite land. The Buddha-land that he sought to establish was vast in extent, unsurpassed, and supremely wonderful, **always present and subject neither to decay nor change**. During inconceivable and innumerable kalpas, he cultivated the immeasurable meritorious practices of the bodhisattva path."[74]*

Then, Ananda asked Shakyamuni a direct and very important question for us:

"Ananda asked the Buddha, 'Has Bodhisattva Dharmakara already attained Buddhahood and then passed into Nirvana? Or has He not yet attained Buddhahood? Or is He dwelling somewhere at present?'

*The Buddha replied to Ananda, 'Bodhisattva Dharmakara has already attained Buddhahood and **is now dwelling** in a Western Buddha- land called 'Peace and Bliss,' a hundred thousand kotis of lands away from here.'*
Ananda further asked the Buddha, 'How much time has passed since He attained Buddhahood?"

http://www.amida-ji-retreat-temple-romania.blogspot.ro
[74] *The Three Pure Land Sutras - A Study and Translation from Chinese* by Hisao Inagaki in collaboration with Harold Stewart, Bukkyo Dendo Kyokai and Numata Center for Buddhist Translation and Research, Kyoto, 2003, p.22.

The Buddha replied, "Since He attained Buddhahood about ten kalpas[75] have passed."'[76]

In the *Smaller Amida Sutra*[77], Shakyamuni also said to Sariputra on the same topic:

*"The Buddha then said to Elder Sāriputra: 'If you travel westward from here, passing a hundred thousand kotis of Buddha-lands, you will come to the land called Utmost Bliss, where there is a Buddha named Amitayus. **He is living there now**, teaching the Dharma'".*[78]

As Shakyamuni confirms, Dharmakara already attained Buddhahood, and from then on in the *Larger Sutra* or the *Smaller Sutra* and *Contemplation Sutra*, He no longer calls Him by this name, but "Amitayus", which means Infinite Life or "Amitabha" - "Infinite Light". **These two aspects, "Infinite Life" (Amitayus) and "Infinite Light" (Amitabha) are merged into the word "Amida"[79], which means the Buddha of Infinite Life and Infinite Light**. His Infinite Life is the effect of the 13th Vow which he made when He was Dharmakara Bodhisattva, while the Infinite Light is the effect of the 12th Vow. So, we cannot separate Amitayus (Infinite Life) from Amitabha (Infinite Light) because these are the two aspects of the same Buddha. In the section 4 from the *Smaller Amida Sutra*, Shakyamuni explained this to Sariputra:

"For what reason, Sāriputra, do you think that Buddha is called Amitabha? Sāriputra, the Buddha's light shines boundlessly and

---

[75] In the section 4 of the *Smaller Amida Sutra,* Shakyamuni also said to Sariputra: *"ten kalpas have passed since Amitāyus attained Enlightenment".*

[76] *The Three Pure Land Sutras - A Study and Translation from Chinese* by Hisao Inagaki in collaboration with Harold Stewart, Bukkyo Dendo Kyokai and Numata Center for Buddhist Translation and Research, Kyoto, 2003, p.23-24.

[77] The *Smaller Amida Sutra* was preached at a different time and location – the Jeta Grove of Anathapindada's Garden in Sravasti.

[78] *The Three Pure Land Sutras - A Study and Translation from Chinese* by Hisao Inagaki in collaboration with Harold Stewart, Bukkyo Dendo Kyokai and Numata Center for Buddhist Translation and Research, Kyoto, 2003, p.103.

[79] Chin / O-Mi-T'o-Fo; Jpn / Amida; Vn / A-Di-Đà. The word "Amitabha" is also used in English to represent both "Amitabha" ("Infinite Light") and "Amitayus" ("Infinite Life"). (T. Cleary).

without hindrance over all the worlds of the ten directions. It is for this reason that He is called Amitabha. Again, Sariputra, the lives of the Buddha and the people of His land last for innumerable, unlimited, and incalculable kalpas. It is for this reason that the Buddha is called Amitayus. "[80]

Shakyamuni tells us another important aspect about Dharmakara who became Amida Buddha – he *"is now dwelling in a Western Buddha-land called 'Peace and Bliss,'"* – which is to be found **not here**, but *"a hundred thousand kotis[81] of lands away from here"*.

This is extremely important, as it shows that there is a clear distinction between this world with its unenlightened beings, and the Pure Land. Shakyamuni did not explain Amida and His Pure Land in ultimate terms, and did not say that they are to be found in one's heart/mind or "here and now", as some nowadays deluded scholars are trying to convince us. On the contrary, Dharmakara who became Amida Buddha is dwelling in His Pure Land, outside of this samsaric realm.

Next, the fact that Amida is **"now dwelling"** in His Pure Land, also shows that He is active now in bringing all beings to His realm. This **now** is everlasting and is referring both to the time when Shakyamuni delivered that discourse (sutra) and also to the time of Shan-tao, Honen, Shinran, Rennyo, we in the XXI century and the future generations that will come after us. Amida is a Buddha of the present in the sense that He has already attained Buddhahood and will act forever for the salvation of all beings. We must not forget that Amida is also the Buddha of "Infinite Life", so for Him, **now** is without end.

But Shakyamuni did more than simply presenting the story of Dharmakara becoming Amida. In order to show that people must accept the existence of this great Buddha, and of His Enlightened

---

[80] *The Three Pure Land Sutras - A Study and Translation from Chinese* by Hisao Inagaki in collaboration with Harold Stewart, Bukkyo Dendo Kyokai and Numata Center for Buddhist Translation and Research, Kyoto, 2003, p.104-105.

[81] Koti is a term used in ancient India to express a high numerical value equivalent to one hundred thousand, ten milion, or one hundred milion.

realm, He actually revealed them to His audience. Here is what happened:

*"The Buddha said to Ananda, 'Rise to your feet, rearrange your robes, put your palms together, and respectfully revere and worship Amitayus.' [...] Ananda stood up, rearranged his robes, assumed the correct posture, faced westward, and, demonstrating his sincere reverence, joined his palms together, prostrated himself on the ground, and worshiped Amitayus. Then he said to Śhakyamuni Buddha, 'World-honored One, **I wish to see that Buddha, His Land of Peace and***
   Bliss, and its hosts of bodhisattvas and sravakas'

*As soon as he had said this, **Amitayus emitted a great light**, which illuminated all the Buddha lands. The Encircling Adamantine Mountains, Mount Sumeru, together with large and small mountains and everything else shone with the same [golden] color. That light was like the flood at the end of the period of cosmic change that fills the whole world, when myriads of things are submerged, and as far as the eye can see there is nothing but the vast expanse of water. Even so was the flood of light emanating from Amitayus. All the lights of sravakas and bodhisattvas were outshone and surpassed, and only the Buddha's light remained shining bright and glorious. At that time **Ananda saw the splendor and majesty of Amitayus** resembling Mount Sumeru, which rises above the whole world. There was no place that was not illuminated by the light emanating from His body of glory [Sambhogakaya or Dharmakaya as compassionate means – Amida's transcendent body]. **The four groups of followers of the Buddha in the assembly saw all this at the same time. Likewise, those of the Pure Land saw everything in this world.***

Then the Buddha said to Ananda and Bodhisattva Maitreya, "Have you seen that land filled with excellent and glorious manifestations, all spontaneously produced, from the ground to the Heaven of the Pure Abode?" Ananda replied, "Yes, I have." The Buddha asked, "Have you also heard the great voice of Amitayus expound the

Dharma to all the worlds, guiding sentient beings to the Way of the Buddha?" Ananda replied, "Yes, I have."[82]

The passage is clear and can't be misinterpreted. Ananda asked Shakyamuni to see Amida and His Pure Land - *"I wish to see that Buddha, His Land of Peace and Bliss"*, and then he actually saw Him – *"Ananda saw the splendor and majesty of Amitayus"*. In fact, not only him, but all those gathered there on Vulture Peak to listen to the *Larger Sutra*, saw Amida and the Pure Land – *"the four groups of followers of the Buddha in the assembly saw all this at the same time"*. Both those in this world and those in the Pure Land, saw each other – *"likewise, those of the Pure Land saw everything in this world"*.

No sincere follower and reader of the above lines can possibly misinterpret what happened there. The revelation of Amida and His Land really took place, and the audience literally saw them before their very eyes. There is no hidden, metaphorical or symbolical meaning in this. I repeat, **the audience literally saw them before their very eyes**. Anybody who tells you that you should not actually take into consideration this vision of Amida and His Land, as it was described in the sutra, is a person who lacks faith and who is consciously or unconsciously deceiving you.

Not only that Shakyamuni showed Amida and the Pure Land to the audience, but He also asked them to confirm what they saw and heard:

"Have you seen that land filled with excellent and glorious manifestations, all spontaneously produced?"

To this, Ananda replied, *"Yes, I have"*.

"Have you also heard the great voice of Amitayus?"

---

[82] *The Three Pure Land Sutras - A Study and Translation from Chinese* by Hisao Inagaki in collaboration with Harold Stewart, Bukkyo Dendo Kyokai and Numata Center for Buddhist Translation and Research, Kyoto, 2003, p.65-66.

Ananda, also replied:

"Yes, I have".

Why do you think Shakyamuni Buddha asked them to confirm what they just saw and heard? Why He insisted to hear Ananda say with his own mouth, "yes I have seen" and "yes, I have heard"? It is because He wanted all beings, including us, disciples of later generations, to accept Amida as a real Buddha, and His Land as a real enlightened place where we should wish to go after death. It was for our sake that He told the story of Amida Buddha and enabled the audience to see Him and His Land:

"I have expounded this teaching (sutra) for the sake of sentient beings and enabled you to see Amitayus (Amida) and all in his Land. Strive to do what you should. After I have passed into Nirvana, do not allow doubt to arise."[83]

According to the *Contemplation Sutra*, Amida Buddha and His Pure Land were also shown to Queen Vaidehi, wife of King Bimbisara from Magadha[84]. Ananda and Mahamaudgalyayana, two

---

[83] *Idem.*, p.70

[84] According to the story of this sutra, the queen and her husband were imprisoned by their son Ajatasatru, at the advice of Devadatta. Out of despair, the queen faced towards the place where Shakyamuni was staying at that moment and prayed that He send two of His major disciples to comfort her. Shakyamuni did this immediately, and He himself came to her through the air. The teaching He gave to the queen has been known since then as the *Sutra on Visualization of the Buddha of Infinite Life* (in short, the *Contemplation Sutra*):

"Vaidehi, thus confined, grew emaciated with grief and despair. Facing Vulture Peak, she worshiped the Buddha from afar and said, "O Tathagata, World-honored One, you used to send Ananda to comfort me. Now I am in deep sorrow and distress. Since there is no way of my coming to look upon your august countenance, World-honored One, I pray you send Venerable Mahamaudgalyayana and Venerable Ananda here to see me."
When she had said these words, tears of sorrow streamed down her cheeks like rain. Then she bowed toward the Buddha in the distance. Even before she raised her head, the World-honored One, who was then staying on Vulture Peak, knew Vaidehi's thoughts and immediately ordered Mahamaudgalyayana and Ananda to

of His main disciples, were themselves present as witnesses of this revelation. Here are the words of this sacred text:

"I [Vaidehi] beseech you, World-honored One, **to reveal to me a land of no sorrow and no affliction where I can be reborn**. I do not wish to live in this defiled and evil world of Jambudvipa where there are hells, realms of hungry ghosts, animals, and many vile beings. I wish that in the future I shall not hear evil words or see wicked people. World-honored One, I now kneel down to repent and beg you to take pity on me.'

Then the World-honored One sent forth from between his eyebrows a flood of light that was the color of gold and illuminated the innumerable worlds in the ten directions. Returning to the Buddha, the light settled on His head and transformed itself into a golden platform resembling Mount Sumeru. On the platform appeared the pure and resplendent lands of all the Buddhas in the ten directions. [...] Innumerable Buddha lands like these, glorious and beautiful, were displayed to her.

Vaideii then said to the Buddha, 'O World-honored One, these Buddha-lands are pure and free of defilement, and all of them are

---

go to her through the air; ***He himself disappeared from the mountain and reappeared in the inner chamber of the royal palace".***

Rennyo Shonin explained that at the time Vaidehi made her request, Shakyamuni Buddha was preaching the *Lotus Sutra* on Vulture Peak:

"Long ago, when Shakyamuni expounded the Lotus Sutra, the wondrous text of the One Vehicle, on Vulture Peak, Devadatta provoked Ajatasatru to acts of treachery; Shakyamuni then led Vaidehi to aspire to the Land of Serene Sustenance. Because Shakyamuni withdrew from the assembly gathered at Vulture Peak where He was expounding the Lotus Sutra, descended to the royal palace, and graciously set forth the Pure Land teaching for Vaidehi's sake, Amida's Primal Vow has flourished to this day. This is why we say that the teachings of the Lotus and the nembutsu were given at the same time".
(*Rennyo Shonin Ofumi: The Letters of Rennyo*, IV-3, BDK English Tripitaka Series, Numata Center for Buddhist Translation and Research, p. 104)

*resplendent. But **I wish to be born in the Land of Utmost Bliss of Amitāyus***'.*"[85]

[...]*"Vaidehi said to the Buddha, "World-honored One, through the Buddha's power, even I have now been able **to see** that land'".*[86]

[...] *"The Buddha said to Ananda and Vaidehi, 'Listen carefully, listen carefully and ponder deeply. I will expound for you the method of removing suffering. Bear my words in mind and explain them to the multitude of beings.'*

*When these words were spoken, **Amitayus appeared in the air above, attended on His left and right by the two mahasattvas Avalokitesvara and Mahasthamaprapta**. So brilliant was their radiance that it was impossible to see them in detail. They could not be compared even with a hundred thousand nuggets of gold from the Jambu River.*

*After **she had this vision of Amitayus**, Vaidehi knelt down in worship at Shakyamuni's feet and said to Him, "World-honored One, **through your power I have been able to see Amitayus and the two Bodhisattvas**".*[87]

After the *Contemplation Sutra* was delivered to Queen Vaidehi, Shakyamuni Buddha returned with His companions to the Vulture Peak. There, Ananda told the audience all that happened, including the vision with Amida Buddha and His Pure Land:

"Then the World-honored One returned to Vulture Peak through the air. There Ananda fully explained to the assembly what had happened. Innumerable humans, devas, nagas, yaksas, and all other beings greatly rejoiced to hear the Buddha's teaching".[88]

---

[85] *The Three Pure Land Sutras - A Study and Translation from Chinese* by Hisao Inagaki in collaboration with Harold Stewart, Bukkyo Dendo Kyokai and Numata Center for Buddhist Translation and Research, Kyoto, 2003, p.70-71
[86] *Idem.*, p.79.
[87] *Idem.*, p.83-84.
[88] *Idem.*, p.100.

As disciples who read and hear this teaching, long after Shakyamuni *"passed into Nirvana"*, we must be on guard against those false teachers and deluded scholars who are incapable of accepting the story of Dharmakara becoming Amida as it was told by Shakyamuni, and the testimony of Ananda, Mahamaudgalyayana, queen Vaidehi and the entire audience from the Vulture Peak who literary saw Amida Buddha and His Pure Land. No matter what nice or sophisticated words such people might use, we must by no means, be confused by them. If Shakyamuni, in His all-knowing wisdom as a Buddha, would have thought there is a better way to explain to us the Dharma about Amida Buddha, then He would surely chose it, but He didn't.

So great is the importance of Amida Dharma and the *Larger Sutra*, that Shakyamuni promised to keep it in the world even after all the other sutras would disappear:

"In the future, the Buddhist scriptures and teachings will perish. But, out of pity and compassion, I will especially preserve this sutra and maintain it in the world for a hundred years more. Those beings who encounter it will attain deliverance in accord with their aspirations".[89]

His urge to listen and accept it in faith is overwhelming:

"Even if a great fire were to fill the universe of a thousand million worlds, you should pass through it to hear this sutra, to arouse joyful faith, to uphold and chant it, and to practice in accordance with its teachings".[90]

How can one dare to say this sutra does not contain the true story of Amida Buddha, when Shakyamuni himself said that even if the universe is on fire, we should by all means, accept it in faith? When all the Masters of our lineage accepted it, how can we say otherwise?

---

[89] *Idem*, p.70.
[90] *Idem.*, p-69-70

However, Shakyamuni foresaw the inner and outer difficulties of accepting this sutra:

"Most difficult of all difficulties is to hear this sutra, have faith in it with joy, and hold fast to it. Nothing is more difficult than this"[91]

It is extremely important to understand that Amida Dharma is what Shakyamuni expounded and taught. This is why He said at the end of the *Larger Sutra*: *"thus have I formed my Dharma, thus have I expounded my Dharma, thus have I taught my Dharma"*. It means, "Dear disciples, do not let yourself drawn into confusion! This is the Dharma you should accept - in the exact way I myself formed it and expounded it". This is also evident from the next sentence: *"you must receive it and practice it by the method prescribed"*.

Attention, dear readers – Shakyamuni said we must receive it and practice it in the way it was taught. Not to change it like we are some kind of owners of the Dharma or enlightened beings ourselves. So please, do not approach the Amida Dharma with a possessive mind, but with the humbleness of receiving the most precious medicine.

---

[91] *Idem.*, p.70

The doctrine of the Three Buddha-Bodies and Two Buddha-Bodies in relation with Amida Buddha and His Pure Land

The Masters of our school used two doctrines or two ways of explaining Amida Buddha and His Pure Land, both admitting as true the story told by Shakyamuni in the *Larger Sutra*. These are called, the Three Buddha-Bodies (Aspects) and the Two Buddha-Bodies doctrines.

The doctrine of the Three Buddha-Bodies (Trikaya):

1. Dharmakaya (Hosshin) or Dharma-Body

This is the aspect of ultimate Reality or the Absolute Truth. It is beyond forms, unchanging, inconceivable, without beginning and no end. All Buddhas share the same Dharmakaya when they attain perfect Enlightenment; this is why it is said that all Buddhas, including Amida, have the same essence. Not only Amida Buddha, but His Pure Land too, has the same Dharmakaya aspect. This is evident from this and many other similar passages in the sacred texts:

My land, being like Nirvana itself,
Will be beyond comparison."[92]

2. Sambhogakaya (Hojin) or Recompensed Body

This is Amida Buddha and His Pure Land in transcendental form, as a result of Dharmakara's practices and Vows. It is called, the "Body of Recompense" because it is the effect, or the "recompense" of His practices and virtues. Thus, when Dharmakara became Amida Buddha, His 48 vows have become effective methods of salvation, and His Pure Land came into existence. To Amida in Sambhogakaya form, did Shakyamuni refer to when He said to Ananda:

---

[92] *The Three Pure Land Sutras - A Study and Translation from Chinese* by Hisao Inagaki in collaboration with Harold Stewart, Bukkyo Dendo Kyokai and Numata Center for Buddhist Translation and Research, Kyoto, 2003, p.9-10

"Bodhisattva Dharmakara has already attained Buddhahood and **is now dwelling** *in a Western Buddha- land called 'Peace and Bliss,' a hundred thousand kotis of lands away from here.'*

[…] Since He attained Buddhahood about ten kalpas have passed."[93]

or when He said to Sariputra:

"The Buddha then said to Elder Sariputra: 'If you travel westward from here, passing a hundred thousand kotis of Buddha-lands, you will come to the land called Utmost Bliss, where there is a Buddha named Amitayus. **He is living there now**, *teaching the Dharma'".*[94]

and also when He described the two aspects of Amida ("Amitabha" – "Infinite Light" and "Amitayus" – "Infinite Life"):

"For what reason, Sariputra, do you think that Buddha is called Amitabha? Sariputra, the Buddha's light shines boundlessly and without hindrance over all the worlds of the ten directions. It is for this reason that He is called Amitabha. Again, Sariputra, the lives of the Buddha and the people of His land last for innumerable, **unlimited**, *and incalculable kalpas. It is for this reason that the Buddha is called Amitayus."*[95]

These aspects are also described in Amida's 12th Vow:

"If, when I attain Buddhahood, **my light should be limited**, *unable to illuminate at least a hundred thousand kotis of nayutas of Buddhalands, may I not attain perfect Enlightenment."*
(the 12th Vow)

and the 13th Vow:

---

[93] *Idem*, p.23-24.
[94] *Idem*, p.103.
[95] *Idem*, p.104-105.

*"If, when I attain Buddhahood, **my life-span should be limited**, even to the extent of a hundred thousand kotis of nayutas of kalpas may I not attain perfect Enlightenment."*

The Infinite (Unlimited) Light of Amida is a transcendent (Sambhogakaya) manifestation capable of going anywhere in the universe. This is why He said that if His *"light should be limited"* then He will not attain Buddhahood. This Light embraces, protects and brings the wisdom of faith (shinjin) into the hearts and minds of people who are open to His message of salvation. Through His Light, Amida tries permanently to influence beings and make them accept His salvation contained in the Primal Vow (18th). It is like an immense magnet attracting all beings to Him. Some become opened to it sooner, while others will do so in the future, but Amida will continue sending it until all hells are empty and all beings will become Buddhas.

The Infinite (Unlimited) Life of Amida simply means that His transcendent (Sambhogakaya) manifestation will last forever for the benefit of all beings. This is why He said that if His *"life-span should be limited"*, then He will not attain Buddhahood. Thus, the Sambhogakaya aspect of Amida Buddha has a beginning, when He attained Buddhahood, and no end (no limit), because He is the Buddha of Infinite (Unlimited) Life[96].

---

[96] I make a difference between eternal" and „unlimited". Only the Dharmakaya aspect of Amida Buddha is eternal, because it has no begining and no end, while His Sambhogakaya aspect has a begining, but will have no end – will be **„unlimited"**, as the sutra said. Shinran Shonin too, emphasized this aspect of unlimitedness of Amida as Sambhogakaya:

*"The life of Amida **is infinite, no measure** can be taken"*
(*Hymn of the Nembutsu and True Shinjin – Passages on the Pure Land Way - The Collected Works of Shinran*, Shin Buddhism Translation Series, Jodo Shinshu Hongwanji-ha, Kyoto, 1997, p. 304)

"Since attainment of Buddhahood, ten kalpas have passed;
*The Buddha's life indeed **has no measure**.*
Shining on the blind and ignorant of the world; hence, I bow in homage".

Also the Infinite (Unlimited) Life of Amida means that He will have enough patience and enough time to help all beings. This Vow is in accord with the well known Mahayana verse:

"As long as space endures and unenlightened beings exist,
may I too remain to dispel the miseries of the world".

So, Amida's Infinite (Unlimited) Life stands for Infinite Compassion. He will make no discrimination among those to be saved, and He will endlessly work to save all beings, without any small break in His activity, as He himself promised:

"If I should not become a great benefactor
In lives to come for immeasurable kalpas
To save the poor and the afflicted everywhere,
May I not attain perfect Enlightenment."[97]

3. Nirmanakaya – Accomodated (Ojin) or Transformed Body (Keshin)

According to Shinran Shonin, this is Amida Buddha as the object of the 9th contemplation (contemplation on the True Body) in the *Contemplation Sutra*. In that contemplation, Shakyamuni describes Amida with a definite measurement or size of the body:

"His (Amida's) body is as glorious as a thousand million kotis of nuggets of gold from the Jambu River of the Yama Heaven and that His height is six hundred thousand kotis of nayutas of yojanas multiplied by the number of the sands of the Ganges River".[98]

(*Hymns of the Pure Land - The Collected Works of Shinran*, Shin Buddhism Translation Series, Jodo Shinshu Hongwanji-ha, Kyoto, 1997, p. 321)
[97] *Larger Sutra,* chapter 8, *The Three Pure Land Sutras - A Study and Translation from Chinese* by Hisao Inagaki in collaboration with Harold Stewart, Bukkyo Dendo Kyokai and Numata Center for Buddhist Translation and Research, Kyoto, 2003, p.20
[98] *The Three Pure Land Sutras - A Study and Translation from Chinese* by Hisao Inagaki in collaboration with Harold Stewart, Bukkyo Dendo Kyokai and Numata Center for Buddhist Translation and Research, Kyoto, 2003, p.86

Thus, in chapter VI of his *Kyogyoshinsho*, Shinran said:

"As I reverently reveal the Transformed Buddha and Land, the Buddha is as described in the
Sutra on Visualisation of the Buddha of Infinite Life [Contemplation Sutra], namely the 'Buddha in the contemplation on the True Body'".[99]

In the same section with the 9th contemplation, the aureole of Amida Buddha is said to contain many *"transformed Buddhas numbering as many as a million kotis of nayutas multiplied by the number of the sands of the Ganges River"*.

These transformed (accommodated) bodies of Amida Buddha, who emerge from His Sambhogakaya aspect, and who vary in sizes and forms, according to the needs and characteristics of beings (this is what is meant by "Accomodated Body"), are sent toward all those in the ten directions of Samsara who entrust to Him, as it is clear from the section 21 of the *Contemplation Sutra:*

"Amitayus, exercising supernatural powers at will, **can freely manifest His various forms in the lands of the ten directions**. *At times He may appear as a large figure, filling the whole sky; at other times as a smaller figure, only sixteen or eight feet high. The figures that He manifests are all of the color of pure gold. The* **transformed Buddhas** *and jeweled lotus flowers in the aureole of each manifested form are like those described above."*[100]

The same is described within this passage:

---

[99] Shinran Shonin, *Kyogyoshinsho*, cf with *Kyogyoshinsho – On Teaching, Practice, Faith, and Enlightenment*, translated by Hisao Inagaki, Numata Center for Buddhist Translation and Research, Kyoto, 2003, p. 233. and *Kygyoshinsho*, Ryukoku Translation Series, Ryukoku University, Kyoto, 1966, p. 161.
[100] *The Three Pure Land Sutras - A Study and Translation from Chinese* by Hisao Inagaki in collaboration with Harold Stewart, Bukkyo Dendo Kyokai and Numata Center for Buddhist Translation and Research, Kyoto, 2003, p.91

"Buddha Amitayus possesses eighty-four thousand physical characteristics, each having eighty-four thousand secondary marks of excellence. Each secondary mark emits eighty-four thousand rays of light; each ray of light shines universally upon the lands of the ten directions, embracing and not forsaking those who are mindful of the Buddha. It is impossible to describe in detail these rays of light, physical characteristics, and marks, transformed Buddhas, and so forth."[101]

Shinran Shonin also believed that one of the many Nirmanakayas or Transformed Bodies of Amida Buddha is Shakyamuni Buddha himself:

"Amida, who attained Buddhahood in the infinite past,
Full of compassion for foolish beings of the five defilements,
Took the form of Sakyamuni Buddha
And appeared in Gaya."[102]

*

In the conclusion of this presentation of Trikaya doctrine, we can say that Amida Buddha is beyond any form in His Dharmakaya aspect dwells with His transcendent form (Sambhogakaya) in the Pure Land, and in the same time He is here with us, people who have genuine faith in Him, in His various Accomodated and Transformation Bodies (Nirmanakayas). Wherever we are, in our room, on the street, alone or with friends and family, etc, Amida Buddha is always accompanying us.

When we ourselves attain Buddhahood in the Pure Land, we'll have access to the ultimate reality beyond forms (Dharmakaya), we'll dwell forever in transcendent form (Sambhogakaya) in Amida's Pure Land, and in the same way, we'll go in all the places of the universe

---

[101] *The Three Pure Land Sutras - A Study and Translation from Chinese* by Hisao Inagaki in collaboration with Harold Stewart, Bukkyo Dendo Kyokai and Numata Center for Buddhist Translation and Research, Kyoto, 2003, p. 87
[102] Shoshinge. *The Way of Nembutsu-Faith: A Commentary on the Shoshinge*, by Hisao Inagaki, Nagata Bunshodo, Kyoto, 1996.

in various Bodies of Accomodation or Transformation (Nirmanakayas) to save all beings.

The doctrine of the Two Buddha-Bodies (Nishu Hosshin)

This doctrine was much explained by Master T'an-luan in his *Ojoronchu*[103]. According to him, all Buddhas, including Amida, have two Bodies/Aspects:

1. Dharmakaya of Dharma-nature (Hossho Hosshin)
2. Dharmakaya of Expediency (Hoben Hosshin), which is also called **"Dharmakaya of Compassionate means".**

The first is the ultimate, unconditioned reality beyond form, which is equally shared by all Buddhas[104], while the second is the specific and particular manifestation of each Buddha for the sake of saving sentient beings.

The relation between the two is described as follows:

"From the Dharmakaya of Dharma-nature originates the Dharmakaya of Expediency; through the Dharmakaya of Expediency, the Dharmakaya of Dharma nature is revealed. These two Dharmakayas are different, but inseparable; they are one but not the same."

The relation between the Doctrine of the "Two Buddha bodies" as expressed by T'an-luan, and the "Three Buddha bodies" (Trikaya)

---

[103] All quotes in this chapter were taken from *"Ojoronchu – T'an-luan's Commentary on Vasubandhu's Discourse on the Pure Land*, A Study and Translation" by Hisao Inagaki, Nagata Bunshodo, Kyoto, 1998.
[104] T'an-luan said: *"All Buddhas Tathagatas are called 'equally enlightened ones'"*. Master Shan-tao said: *"All Buddhas have attained one and the same Enlightenment"*. Also in the *Garland Sutra*, quoted by Shinran Shonin in his *Kyogyoshinsho*, it is said: *"The bodies of all Buddhas are only one Dharma.body"*.

79

The Dharmakaya of Dharma-nature is identical with the Dharmakaya reffered to in the Trikaya doctrine, and the Dharmakaya of Expediency (Dharmakaya of Compassionate means) corresponds to the Sambhogakaya or Recompensed Body[105]. Nirmanakaya or various Transformed Bodies are manifested/emanated from Sambhogakaya and thus, we can consider it as part of the Dharmakaya of Expediency.

Shinran Shonin accepted both explanations of the Bodies (Aspects) of Amida Buddha, as we can see in this verse from his *Jodo Wasan*:

"It is taught that ten kalpas have now passed
Since Amida attained Buddhahood,
   (Three Buddha Bodies doctrine)

But He seems a Buddha more ancient
Than kalpas countless as particles."[106]
   (Two Buddha Bodies doctrine)

In the first two verses Amida is described as Dharmakaya of Expediency or Dharmakaya for the sake of sentient beings (Sambhogakaya), while in the last verses His ultimate formless Dharmakaya (Dharmakaya of Dharma-nature) is revealed.

Both Shinran and T'an-luan did not deny the story of Bodhisattva Dharmakara becoming Amida ten kalpas ago, as described in the *Larger Sutra*[107] – *"it is taught that ten kalpas have now passed since*

---

[105] Nirmanakaya or Transformed Body is included in the Sambhogakaya and thus, it is part of the Dharmakaya of Expediency.

[106] *The Collected Works of Shinran*, Shin Buddhism Translation Series, Jodo Shinshu Hongwanji-ha, Kyoto, 1997, p.349

[107] Master T'an-luan accepted the story of Dharmakara becoming Amida from the *Larger Sutra*, and also emphasized that when Dharmakara decided to work for the creation of the Pure Land, he was not an ordinary Bodhisattva or monk, but one who actually had nothing more to do for his own liberation. Here are a few important passages from his *Ojoronchu*:

"Formerly, in the presence of Lokesvararaja Buddha, Dharmakara Bodhisattva attained insight into the non-arising of all dharmas. This stage is called the Sage's

Amida attained Buddhahood" – but they also wished to point out that this is only one aspect of Amida, namely Dharmakaya of Expediency/Sambhogakaya, and that He also has an ultimate Buddha nature (Dharmakaya of Dharma-nature) which has no beginning and no end: *"He seems a Buddha more ancient than kalpas* **countless** *as particles."*

This ultimate aspect of Amida, or Amida as a Dharmakaya Buddha, is the essence and true nature of His transcendental manifestations or Amida as Sambhogakaya Buddha. Thus, **Amida as Dharmakaya is preceding Amida as a result of Bodhisattva Dharmakara practices and vows (Amida as described in the *Larger Sutra*).** Why do I say this? The reason is very simple – **Amida as Dharmakaya is the same with Suchness[108], Nirvana or Buddha nature, which is always present (without beginning and without end) and not produced by anything, while Amida as Sambhogakaya, or Amida as Dharmakaya of Expediency, has a beginning in the moment Dharmakara fulfilled His practices and attained Enlightenment.**

This is why the Buddhas are called Tathagatas. The term," Tathagata" is composed of "tathā" and "āgata, which means "thus come", or "tathā" and "gata", which means "thus gone". The term refers to a Buddha who has "thus gone" from Samsara into

---

Family. While dwelling there, he made the Forty-eight Great Vows, whereby he was able to provide his Land called ,Peace and Bliss'. This means that this Land is the result of that cause."

[...] "The Pure Land of Peace and Bliss has indeed arisen from the pure karma of the Bodhisattva Dharmakara, who had attained an insight into the unproduced nature of all dharmas. It is also the realm ruled by the Dharma-King Amida. Indeed, the Tathagata Amida provided the controlling power in the formation and support of the Pure Land."

[...] "The Land of Peace and Bliss was produced by through Dharmakara Bodhisattva's Compassion and Right Meditation. It was established by Amida Tathagata's Divine Power and Primal Vow."

[108] Sometimes the term is Thusness instead of Suchness. Both indicate the same ultimate reality.

Nirvana/Suchness, but also who has "thus come" from Nirvana/Suchness to work for the salvation of all sentient beings. In our case, Amida as Dharmakaya of Dharma-nature is Nirvana/Suchness itself, as Shinran said:

"Supreme Nirvana is the uncreated dharma-body. Uncreated dharma-body is true reality. True reality is dharma-nature. Dharma nature is Suchness. Suchness is Oneness. **Amida Tathagata comes forth from Suchness and manifests various bodies – fulfilled (Sambhogakaya/Dharmakaya of Expediency), accommodated and transformed**"*.[109]*

So, when Dharmakara attained perfect Enlightenment/Nirvana/Suchness, He automatically became Amida Tathagata in two aspects: 1) Amida as Dharmakaya or ultimate reality beyond forms, with no beginning and no end ("Thus Gone"), and 2) Amida as Dharmakaya of Expediency or Sambhogakaya, that is Amida in Form and Name, dwelling in His Pure Land ("Thus Come"). Both are different aspects of the one and the same Amida Buddha, but again, if we ask ourselves, who was first, Amida as Dharmakaya or Amida as Sambhogakaya, we should answer – Amida as Dharmakaya. This is because, as I said above, **the ultimate Dharmakaya is always present; it was present before Bodhisattva Dharmakara formulated the 48 vows and started the practices, before He attained Enlightenment and became Amida, and will always be present in the never ending future. This is the logic of Shinran's words,** *"He seems a Buddha more ancient than kalpas countless as particles"* and of the Two Buddha Bodies Doctrine according to which Amida as Dharmakaya of Dharma-nature (Amida beyond form) is the origin and essence (the true nature) of Amida as Dharmakaya of Expediency (Amida in Form and Name/Amida in His Pure Land).

Without Dharmakara becoming Amida in Sambhogakaya form (Dharmakaya of Expediency), Amida as Dharmakaya beyond form

---

[109] *The Collected Works of Shinran*, Shin Buddhism Translation Series, Jodo Shinshu Hongwanji-ha, Kyoto, 1997, p.153.

could not save anybody. So, we say as Master T'an-luan: *"from the Dharmakaya of Dharma nature originates the Dharmakaya of Expediency"*.

Also, without Amida in His eternal aspect beyond form, there is no Amida in Form and Name, that is, Amida as the Reward of Dharmakara practices and vows. This is because **if Bodhisattva Dharmakara did not awaken himself to the Dharmakaya beyond form, he could not become Dharmakaya in Form and Name or Amida as described in the *Larger Sutra*,** dwelling in His Pure Land. It is very important to understand that **without perfect Enlightenment or Suchness (ultimate Dharmakaya) as its base and true nature, Amida in Form and Name and His Pure Land would be just another samsaric manifestation**[110]. This is why, Master T'an-luan used the term **Dharmakaya** for both the ultimate nature of Amida Buddha (**Dharmakaya** of Dharma-nature) and for His transcendent manifestations (**Dharmakaya** of Expediency) – he wanted us to know that the last are firmly grounded in the ultimate, formless Dharmakaya.

So, again, when Bodhisattva Dharmakara attained perfect Enlightenment, He awoke himself to the ever-existent and non-produced Dharmakaya beyond form. In that moment, and in accord with His 48 Vows, Amida in Form and Name and the Pure Land came into existence. **The attainment of perfect Enlightenment or Awakening to ultimate Dharmakaya was the decisive factor who produced the Sambhogakaya (Dharmakaya of Expediency) aspect of Amida and His Pure Land. This again, is the logic of saying, *"from the Dharmakaya of Dharma nature originates the Dharmakaya of Expediency"*.** From Awakening to the ever-present Dharmakaya/Suchness/Buddha-nature/Nirvana, and on the basis of this Awakening, originates the transcendent manifestations for the sake of saving sentient beings, which is Amida in Form and Name, and His Pure Land.

---

[110] The land of Amida is itself in accord with ultimate Dharmakaya or Dharmakaya of Dharma-nature:
„*This Pure Land complies with the Dharma- nature and is not in conflict with the Dharma-base*".

83

In short, **Amida as ultimate Dharmakaya is the "*Buddha more ancient than kalpas countless as particles*"**, as Shinran said, and Amida in Sambhogakaya form or Amida as Dharmakaya of Expediency is His manifestation in accord with Dharmakara's practices and vows. **What the *Larger Sutra* shows to us, is the process through which Amida as ultimate Dharmakaya becomes Amida in Form and Name for the sake of saving sentient beings.** This process was perfected ten kalpas ago, as Shakyamuni and Shinran Shonin explained, *"ten kalpas have now passed since Amida attained Buddhahood"*.

The two aspects of the Pure Land

The Pure Land of Amida Buddha has two main aspects: 1) the ultimate Dharmakaya aspect, and   2) the manifestation or Sambhogakaya (recompense) aspect.

1) The first aspect (Dharmakaya) means that the Pure Land is Nirvanic in its essence, as it was stated in the *Larger Sutra*:

My land, being like Nirvana itself,
Will be beyond comparison."[111]

This means that all the manifestations of the Pure Land are grounded in the perfect Enlightenment of Amida Buddha, and are conducive to Enlightenment. We ourselves will attain Enlightenment when we are born in the Pure Land, because the essence of the Pure Land is Enlightenment/Nirvana/Dharmakaya itself. Otherwise, if the Pure Land was not an enlightened realm, it would produce only sensorial attachments, like other Samsaric realms do, but Shakyamuni Buddha[112] and our Masters[113] were very clear that this is not the case.

Also, Bodhisattva Vasubandhu stated in his *Jodoron[114]*:

---

[111] *The Three Pure Land Sutras - A Study and Translation from Chinese* by Hisao Inagaki in collaboration with Harold Stewart, Bukkyo Dendo Kyokai and Numata Center for Buddhist Translation and Research, Kyoto, 2003, p.9-10
[112] For example, when He explained the role and origin of the wonderful birds of the Pure Land, Shakyamuni said:

"Shariputra, you should not assume that these birds are born as retribution of their evil karma. The reason is that none of the three evil realms exists in that Buddha-land. Shariputra, even the names of the three evil realms do not exist there; how much less the realms themselves? These birds are manifested by Amida Buddha so that their singing can proclaim and spread the Dharma".

[113] For example, Master T'ao-ch'o said in his *An Le Chi*, „*The streams, birds, and forests all expound the Dharma, which awaken people to the principle of non-arising."*
[114] *Treatise on the Pure Land*, in The Pure Land Writings, vol I – the Indian Masters, Jodo Shinshu Hongwanji-ha, Kyoto, 2012, p. 57

"The adornments of the Land of the Buddha of Immeasurable Life are the wondrous manifestations of the ultimate reality".

And in the *Essentials of Faith Alone*, Master Seikaku said:

"'The Land of Bliss is the realm of Nirvana, the uncreated'.

The "uncreated" refers to ultimate Dharmakaya beyond forms, which is the essence of all Buddhas and their lands. From this Dharmakaya emerge all the manifestations for the sake of saving sentient beings in accordance with the specific vows of different Buddhas. In our case, the Pure Land of Amida appeared when He attained perfect Enlightenment and thus brought His 48 vows to fulfilment. In that moment, His land took the form and manifestations described in the sutras and especially in His 31st and 32nd Vows, while also maintaining its formless Dharmakaya essence.

2) About the Sambhogakaya (Recompense) aspect of the Pure Land, Shinran Shonin said:
"We clearly know from the Tathagata's teaching of truth and the masters' commentaries that the Pure Land of Peace and Provision is the True Land of Recompense".[115]
This is because the Pure Land is the effect or "recompense" of Dharmakara's practices and vows, and it came into existence when Bodhisattva Dharmakara became Amida Buddha:

"When I contemplate "recompense," I find that the accomplished land has resulted as the recompense for the Tathagata's oceanlike Vow. Hence, 'recompensed'."[116]

So, being a Recompensed (Sambhogakaya) Land, the Pure Land is the result or recompense of the fulfilment of the 31st Vow:

---

[115] *Kyogyoshinsho – On Teaching, Practice, Faith, and Enlightenment*, translated by Hisao Inagaki, Numata Center for Buddhist Translation and Research, Kyoto, 2003, p. 229.
[116] Idem., p.230

"If, when I attain Buddhahood, my land should not be resplendent, revealing in its light all the immeasurable, innumerable and inconceivable Buddha-lands, like images reflected in a clear mirror, may I not attain perfect Enlightenment."

And the 32nd Vow:

"If, when I attain Buddhahood, all the myriads of manifestations in my land, from the ground to the sky, such as palaces, pavilions, ponds, streams and trees, should not be composed of both countless treasures, which surpass in supreme excellence anything in the worlds of humans and devas, and of a hundred thousand kinds of aromatic wood, whose fragrance pervades all the worlds of the ten quarters, causing all bodhisattvas who sense it to perform Buddhist practices, then may I not attain perfect Enlightenment."

The Light of the Pure Land is the Light of Amida Buddha, the Pure Land itself being the transcendental manifestation of Amida Buddha. This is why the 31st Vow is closely related with the 12th Vow, showing the unity between Amida as an Enlightened Person and His Pure Land.

The **"myriads of manifestations"** mentioned in the 32nd Vow show that the Pure Land surpasses all other places in the world of suffering – *"surpass in supreme excellence anything in the worlds of humans and devas"*. In fact, the Pure Land is beyond Samsara and cannot be compared with the realms caught in the power of birth and death, thus subject to impermanence. Humans, devas (gods) plus other kinds of sentient beings and the environments in which they are born are the product of their unenlightened karma, but the Pure Land of Amida is the manifestation of His supreme Enlightenment and pure merits, so all its treasures and manifestations are supreme in beauty while in the same time they have the power to deepen and strengthen the dedication of those engaged in the practice of liberating themselves and others (bodhisattvas): *"a hundred thousand kinds of aromatic wood, whose fragrance pervades all the worlds of the ten quarters, causing all bodhisattvas who sense it to perform Buddhist practices."*

It is obvious that the treasures found in the Pure Land are not intended for the enjoyment of the six senses but for expressing the Dharma, calling beings to the Dharma, praising Amida's virtues and showing the supreme place this enlightened land occupies among other Buddha lands. They are spiritual treasures, even if they are described using the terms we are familiar with, like palaces, pavilions, ponds, streams and trees, aromatic wood, etc.

*

Shinran Shonin distinguished between two aspects of Amida's Pure Land as a Recompensed Land (Sambhogakaya):

1) the Fulfilled Pure Land (sometimes named the True Recompensed Land), and
2) the Transformed Pure Land[117]

It is important to emphasize that both are the rewards of the Vows of Amida Buddha, so they are not different realms, but part of the same Recompensed (Sambhogakaya) Pure Land. **This is why I call them two aspects, and not two Pure Lands.**

Those born in the Fulfilled Pure Land are followers of the true faith (shinjin) of the 18th Vow (Primal Vow) and they immediately attain Nirvana or Buddhahood, while those who are born in the Transformed Pure Land are followers of the 19th and 20th Vows. The later are people with mixed faith, and so they need to stay for a while in that place until they overcome their doubts.

As Master Shan-tao called it, birth in the Fulfilled Land of the Pure Land is called *"Inconceivable Birth"* and all those born there *"are endowed with bodies of Naturalness, Emptiness, and Infinity"*[118]. To

---

[117] If we make a correspondence with the Three Buddha Bodies doctrine, we may say that this is the Nirmanakaya aspect of the Pure Land.

[118] *Larger Sutra.* Shinran himself made reference to that passage in *the Larger Sutra*, in his work, *Passages on the Pure Land Way* [REALIZATION]:
"Their countenances are dignified and wonderful, surpassing things of this world. Their features, subtle and delicate, are not those of human beings or devas; all receive the body of naturalness or of emptiness, the body of boundlessness."

88

have bodies of *Naturalness, Emptiness and Infinity* means to become a Buddha or to attain perfect Enlightenment.

The Pure Land in the aspect of the Transformed Land is as described in the "thirteen contemplations" and the "nine grades of aspirants" from the *Contemplation Sutra,* but also in the *Larger Sutra* and other texts. As Shinran explained:

"The Transformed Land refers to the Pure Land as shown in the Contemplation Sutra; again it is as described in the Sutra on the Bodhisattvas Dwelling in the Womb (Bosatsu Shotai Kyo), namely the Realm of Sloth and Pride; again it is as described in the Larger Sutra as the Castle of Doubt and the Womb-Palace."[119]

So, the Border Land (Henji)[120], Realm of Sloth and Pride (Keman)[121], the Castle of Doubt (Gijo)[122], and the Womb-Palace (Taigu)[123] are different names for the Transformed Land aspect of the Pure Land, which is where the followers of the 19th and 20th Vows are born. To recite the Nembutsu in self-power or to do other Buddhist practices to gain birth in Amida's Land, results in not

---

[119] Shinran Shonin, *Kyogyoshinsho,* cf with *Kyogyoshinsho – On Teaching, Practice, Faith, and Enlightenment,* translated by Hisao Inagaki, Numata Center for Buddhist Translation and Research, Kyoto, 2003, p. 233. and *Kygyoshinsho,* Ryukoku Translation Series, Ryukoku University, Kyoto, 1966, p. 162.

[120] It is thus called because those born there are far removed from the true bliss of the Pure Land just as those in a border land are less benefited by civilisation. cf with *Tannisho – Notes Lamenting Differences,* Ryukoku Translation Series, Ryukoku University, Kyoto, 1962, p. 41, fn 1.

[121] It is thus called because those born there are too proud to believe in the Buddha's Primal Vow whole-heartedly, and due to the lack of faith they are not so dilligent as to advance to the True Land of Recompense. cf with *Tannisho – Notes Lamenting Differences,* Ryukoku Translation Series, Ryukoku University, Kyoto, 1962, p. 41, fn 1.

[122] It is thus called because those born there have to stay in the Transformed Land due to the sin of doubting just as though pent up in a castle. cf with *Tannisho – Notes Lamenting Differences,* Ryukoku Translation Series, Ryukoku University, Kyoto, 1962, p. 41, fn 1.

[123] It is thus called because those born there are like being inclosed in a lotus flower and can neither see the Buddha nor hear the Dharma. cf with *Tannisho – Notes Lamenting Differences,* Ryukoku Translation Series, Ryukoku University, Kyoto, 1962, p. 41, fn 1.

entering directly into the centre of the Pure Land (or the Fulfilled Pure Land), but in staying for a while in this Transformed Land. People born there do not immediately attain the state of Buddhahood, like those born in the centre of the Pure Land through the gate of the Primal Vow, but they are also free once and for all from the suffering of birth and death in Samsara. They are safe, but still they are not enlightened. In the same time, being in the special environment of this borderland of the Pure Land they have the opportunity to overcome their doubts and entrust completely in Amida Buddha. When they do this, they also enter the Fulfilled Pure Land and attain Nirvana (perfect Enlightenment) or Buddhahood.

Referring to the Transformed Land (borderland of the Pure Land), Shinran said:

"Since practitioners of shinjin are few, many are guided to the transformed land".

Master Shan-tao also said:

"Those born in the Fulfilled Pure Land are extremely few; those born in the Transformed Pure Land are many."

Again, I stress the importance that both the "Transformed Land" and "the Fulfilled Pure Land" (or "True Land of Recompense") are aspects of the same Pure Land of Amida Buddha, just like the anteroom and the main room are part of the same house. As usually, the owner of the house (in our case – Amida Buddha) prefers to stay in the main room together with His faithful sons (followers of the 18th Vow), while those who have a mixed faith (followers of the 19th and 20th Vows) keep themselves in the anteroom. It is not the fault of Amida or a punishment that some are born in the borderland of the Pure Land (Transformed Land)[124], just they are kept in that region by

---

[124] Birth in the Transformed Pure Land by the followers of the 19th Vow is called *Birth under the Twin Sala Trees"* (Sojuringe Ojo). Birth in the Transformed Pure Land by followers of the 20th Vow is called *"Incomprehensible Birth"* (Nanji Ojo). The word " incomprehensible" is used with two meanings: 1) to praise their

their own doubts. They are the ones who are keeping themselves out of the main room of the Pure Land, not Amida Buddha, so when they overcome their doubts, they will also join the Fulfilled Pure Land and immediately attain Nirvana (Buddhahood).

attainment of Birth in comparison with a lower mode of Birth attained by the followers of the 19th Vow and 2) to depreciate it in comparison with a higher mode of Birth attained by the followers of the 18th Vow.
(*The Kyogyoshinsho*, Ryukoku Translation Center, Ryukoku University, Kyoto, 1966, p.160, fn. 8.)

The karmic consequence of denying the transcendent reality of Amida Buddha and His Pure Land

The Three Buddha Bodies (aspects) and the Two Buddha Bodies doctrines are usually not properly understood by those who don't accept the existence of the many transcendent Buddhas in Mahayana[125]. While the true reason for such an attitude is their materialistic vision of the universe, they often use the formless Dharmakaya (Dharmakaya of Dharma-nature) as an excuse and argument to reduce all transcendent manifestations to mere symbols or metaphors, or even go so far as to blame "folk Buddhism" for their presence in the canonical writings.

But surely, Master T'an-luan did not share such distorted views when he clearly said that exactly **because Dharmakaya is formless, there is no form which it cannot manifest**.

"Unconditioned Dharmakaya is the body of Dharma-nature. Because Dharma-nature is Nirvanic, Dharmakaya is formless. Because it is formless, there is no form which it cannot manifest. Therefore, the body adorned with the marks of excellence is itself Dharmakaya".

"The body adorned with the marks of excellence" is the specific transcendent manifestation of each Buddha for the sake of saving sentient beings:

"The Dharmakaya has no form of its own and yet manifests various forms, corresponding to the conditions and capacities of sentient beings."

In the case of Amida Buddha, this is the Form He has taken in the Pure Land; it is Amida as described in the *Larger Sutra* by Shakyamuni, and as seen and heard by the audience gathered together

---

[125] Master T'an-luan clearly explained: *"To say that each Buddha rules innumerable and incalculable worlds in all the ten directions is a view maintained in Mahayana discourses".*

92

on the Vulture Peak to listen to this sutra. It is Amida who always accompany us, sentient beings who entrust to Him.

Ultimate Dharmakaya or Dharmakaya of Dharma-nature is beyond time and form, so it cannot be perceived as an object of faith. In this ultimate Dharmakaya we dwell only after we attain Buddhahood in the Pure Land, but here and now ordinary unenlightened people like us cannot relate to it, nor understand it. This is why **Amida Buddha does not remain secluded in His ultimate - formless Dharmakaya, but has manifested himself in the form described by Shakyamuni in the *Larger Sutra*, and has established His Pure Land.**

Even if Amida Buddha in Form and Name is inseparable from His formless Dharmakaya, it doesn't mean that He is non-existent or just a symbol or fictional character. As the saying goes, even if the two Dharmakayas are inseparable, they are different; they are one, but not the same. So, **while we accept that Amida has the aspect of ultimate formless Dharmakaya, we relate in our faith and teaching to Amida in Form and Name, to Amida as described in the *Larger Sutra* and to Amida who now resides in the Pure Land. Those who do not understand this difference, but continue to negate the existence of Amida Buddha in Form and Name are not practicing in accord with the Dharma**, as T'an-luan explained:

"What is the cause of not practicing in accord with the Dharma, or in agreement with the significance of the Name?
It is due to failure to understand that the Tathagata Amida is a Body of [ultimate] Reality and a Body for the sake of Living Beings."

When we say the nembutsu, we take as object of our faith and refuge, the Name of Amida Buddha in His glorious manifestation for the sake of saving sentient beings (Dharmakaya of Expediency/Sambhogakaya):
"The ten repetitions of the Name arise from the unsurpassed faith by taking as object the Name of Amida Tathagata of a glorious body of skilful means that comprises immeasurable merits which are true and pure."

93

To negate the existence of transcendent Buddhas, including Amida, with their various manifestations, is, according to T'an-luan, the most evil act of abusing the right Dharma. In a famous dialogue from his *Ojoronchu*, which is later mentioned by Shinran in his *Kyogyoshinsho*, he explains that the only obstacle to birth in the Pure Land and the true exclusion in the Primal Vow is the act of abusing the right Dharma. Then he defines the abusing of the right Dharma as follows:

"If one says , 'there is no Buddha', 'there is no Buddha Dharma', 'there is no Bodhisattva' and 'there is no Dharma for Bodhisattvas', such views held firmly in the mind by one's own reasoning or by listening to other's teaching, are called, 'abusing the right Dharma.'"

Now the thing is that those who consider the story told by Shakyamuni in the *Larger Sutra*, of Dharmakara Bodhisattva becoming Amida Buddha, to be a fictional story, and Dharmakara or Amida to be fictional characters, symbols or metaphors, are actually saying "there was no Dharmakara Bodhisattva" and " there is no Amida Buddha". Their act of denying the existence of Amida Buddha in His Dharmakaya of Expediency (Sambhogakaya form) or the Body (Aspect) for the sake of saving sentient beings, is abusing the right Dharma. For this reason, those who spread such distorted visions are excluded from birth in the Pure Land. More than this, when their present life is over, they will be reborn in the Great Avici Hell, as T'an-luan explained:

"He who has committed the transgression of abusing the right Dharma will not be able to attain Birth, even though he has not committed any other evils. For what reason? The Mahaprajnaparamita[126] sutra says:

[...] Those who have abused the right Dharma will also fall into the Great Avici hell. When the period of one kalpa comes to an end,

---

[126] *Daibonhannyaharamitsukyo.*

they will be sent to the Great Avici hell of another world. In this way, such evildoers will consecutively pass through a hundred thousand Great Avici hells.'

The Buddha thus did not mention the time of their release from the Avici hell. This is because the transgression of abusing the right Dharma is extremely grave.
Further, the right Dharma refers to the Buddha Dharma. Such ignorant persons have abused it; therefore, it does not stand to reason that they should seek birth in a Buddha-land, does it?"

The *Larger Sutra* is the Amida Dharma taught by Shakyamuni Buddha with the intention of helping sentient beings to be born in the Pure Land of Amida. Those who do not take this sutra and Dharma as being genuine, but call it a fictional or mythological story, how can they be reborn in a Pure Land of a Buddha whose existence they actually deny? Indeed, as T'an-luan said, *"it does not stand to reason"*, isn't it ?

A collection of passages on the true meaning of birth in the Pure Land of Amida Buddha

Unfortunately, many people nowadays do not correctly understand the meaning of birth in the Pure Land of Amida Buddha, and explain it in terms that are alien to our school, like being "here and now", or "in our mind[127]", etc; thus denying its actual existence as an Enlightened place and of birth there after death.

The collection of passages from the sacred texts that I am going to present to you in the next pages proves the falsity of such claims and helps us understand the true teaching on birth in the Pure Land. They

---

[127] Chih-i (538-597), the founding master of the Tendai Buddhist school in China, advocated the idea that the Pure Land "exists in one's mind", which was later transmitted to Japan. This can be found in the *Vimalakirti Sutra*, a teaching belonging to a diferent Dharma gate than the Pure Land, and in which it is said that if one's mind is pure then the land appears pure by virtue of the purity of the mind. Essentially speaking, the Pure Land was understood by many Tendai masters of the past as existing only in one's mind. Chih-i even spoke of Amida Buddha and His Pure Land as elements of one's consciousness to be realized in the mind.

Nowadays, many followers and so-called teachers of our school take this idea and integrate it in various ways into their own interpretation of the Jodo Shinshu teaching without knowing or without wanting to accept that such ideas are against the Pure Land teaching advocated by our Founding Masters.

We need to understand very well that contrary to the theories of "mind only" or "pure land is pure mind", the Jodo Shinshu teaching recognizes the existence of many transcendental Buddhas who preside over many realms or Buddha-lands and that it is possible, by various methods, to be born in one of these after death. Various examples of such Buddha-lands are, for example, Maitreya's Tusita Heaven, Akyobhya's land, the land of Tara Bodhisattva, Bhaisajyaguru (Yakushi) Buddha's land and Amida's land of the west, the last mentioned of which is the best land to be born into by those who wish to attain Buddhahood quickly. The real existence of such Buddha-lands and especially of Amida Buddha's Pure Land was naturally accepted by the masters of our school, including Nagarjuna, Shan-tao, Honen, Shinran and others who clearly instructed us to aspire to be born **only** in Amida's Pure Land. They all embraced the idea of the Pure Land from the viewpoint of the next life (raisejodo), which means it is to be attained after physical death. We'll clearly see this in the next pages.

do not recquire special explanations as they are not hard to understand.

To make the lecture easier to follow, I divided the passages in three categories:

1) Passages which show that birth in the Pure Land takes place after death,

2) Passages which show that birth in the Pure Land takes place after death and it means the attainment of Nirvana (Enlightenment/Buddhahood), and

3) Passages which show the enlightened qualities of those born in the Pure Land of Amida, and which can't be found in the "here and now" samsaric bodies and minds of unenlightened followers.

1) Passages which show that birth in the Pure Land takes place after death

When their lives are about to end, Amida Buddha will appear before them with a host of sages. When they die, their minds will not fall into confusion and so they will be born in his land. "[128]

Shinran Shonin, quoted the *Smaller Amida Sutra*, in his *Kyogyoshinsho*

"It is like a wax seal impressed on the clay; as the wax seal is destroyed, the letter is formed. When one's life ends, one is born in the Land of Peace and Bliss."[129]

Master Tao-ch'o, *An-le-chi (Anrakushu)*

*

"If one wholeheartedly places faith in the Buddhist teachings and aspires to be born in the Pure Land, one is born there as soon as one's life—whether short or long—ends. [...]

I now urge you to turn to the Land of Utmost Bliss for refuge. If you dedicate all your practice toward it with sincerity of heart, you will be born there, without fail, after the end of your life.[130]

Master Tao-ch'o, *An-le-chi (Anrakushu)*

*

In his *An-le-chi (Anrakushu)*, Master Tao-ch'o presents the following question:

---

[128] *Kyogyoshinsho – On Teaching, Practice, Faith, and Enlightenment*, translated by Hisao Inagaki, Numata Center for Buddhist Translation and Research, Kyoto, 2003, p. 37.

[129] *Collection of Passages on the Land of Peace and Bliss - AN LE CHI* by Tao-ch'o, translated by Zuio Hisao Inagaki, Horai Association International, Singapore, 2015, p.62

[130] *Idem*, p.97

"Is there scriptural evidence to prove that by aspiring to birth in the Pure Land one can be born there at one's death?"[131]

then he quotes many passages from the various sutras to prove there is indeed such a scriptural evidence. From all the passages he quoted, I am presenting you only a few:

"As the Dharma Drum Sutra states: 'Even though you are unable to be mindful (of the Buddha), if you know that the Buddha dwells in the west and think of attaining birth there, you will be born there.'"[132]

As you can see, *"the Buddha dwells in the west"*, so His Land is there, not "here and now".[133]

---

[131]*Idem*, p.98

[132] *Idem*, p.99

[133] In relation with this, I present to you the following question and my answer.
Question: "Why is the Pure Land of Amida Buddha called "the Western Pure Land" or "the Pure Land of the West"? Why is the "west" so much emphasized in many of the sacred writings related with Amida? And also why is the Pure Land described in such a fantastic way in the sutras?"

Answer: In order to show that Amida's Pure Land is not a metaphor, but a real place in which people can actually aspire to be born after death, the land is given a direction and is described in great details in the sutras.

Some say that the direction "west" and the marvelous descriptions of the Pure Land are a proof for its non-existence or for its existence as a symbol or metaphor only. But the truth is that by making the effort to describe in many words the wonders of the Pure Land and by pointing to a direction where to face the Pure Land when worshipping Amida, Shakyamuni Buddha wants to emphasize its actual existence as a place where sentient beings should aspire to be born without worry and doubt.

It is as though I speak to you about a beautiful park I would like you to visit. If I tell you, "it's there, in the west part of town" and I start describing it to you, then you will have no doubt about its existence and you will wish to see it. It's the same with the expression "Pure Land of the West".

The exaltation with which Shakyamuni describes the Pure Land of Amida in the *Smaller Amida Sutra (Amida-kyo)* without even being asked to do it (*Amida-kyo* is a sutra spontaneously delivered, not in response to a question), or the radiant light

"Again, it is stated in the Great Compassion Sutra (adapted):
'Why is this called 'Great Compassion'? Those who single-mindedly practice the Nembutsu without ceasing will be certainly born in the Land of Pace and Bliss after death. Those who urge the transmission of the Nembutsu from person to person, it should be known, are all those who practice the great compassion.'"[134]

Master Tao-ch'o, *An-le-chi (Anrakushu)*

*

"In the Garland Sutra it is stated:
'By practicing the Nembutsu Samadhi,
one unfailingly sees the Buddha,
and will be born in His presence after death.
So, if you see a man at his deathbed, urge him to say the Nembutsu;
Also show him a Buddha's figure so that he could see and worship it.'"[135]

Master Tao-ch'o, *An-le-chi (Anrakushu)*

*

"Those who are mindful of Amida continuously until the end of their lives will be born in the Pure Land, ten out of ten and a hundred out of a hundred. The reason is that they are free of miscellaneous influences from the outside, they have attained the right mindfulness, they are in accord with the Buddha's Primal Vow, they do not

---

that emanated from His body when He delivered the *Larger Sutra* in which He expounded the story of Amida and His 48th vows, are both an indication that His words were true and His listeners should accept Amida as a living Buddha and His Pure Land as a real place.

[134] *Collection of Passages on the Land of Peace and Bliss - AN LE CHI* by Tao-ch'o, translated by Zuio Hisao Inagaki, Horai Association International, Singapore, 2015, p.100
[135] *Idem* p.89

disagree with the Buddha's teachings, and they accord with the Buddha's words".[136]
Master Shan-tao, *Ojoraisan*

"Mindful of Amida continuously" means that their faith (shinjin) in Amida Buddha is truly settled and so it will not disappear until the end of their lives when the actual birth in the Pure Land takes place. "Right mindfulness" is the faith (shinjin) of the Primal Vow.

*

"Shakyamuni and other Buddhas throughout the ten quarters glorify Amida's Light with twelve names and extensively urge beings to recite the Name and worship Him continuously without interruption, for such people will gain immeasurable merits in this lifetime and, after death, definitely attain birth in the Pure Land".[137]
Master Shan-tao, *Ojoraisan*

*

"If you are to choose the place for birth in the next life,
The Western Land is most suited for you to go".[138]
Master Shan-tao, *Ojoraisan*

*

"Those who continuously recite the Name, as explained above, until the end of their lives, will all be born in the Pure Land, ten out of ten and a hundred out of a hundred. Why? Because such people are free of obstructions from outside and dwell in the state of right mindfulness, and so they are in accord with the Buddha's Primal

---

[136] *Shan-tao's Liturgy for Birth – Ojoraisan*, compiled by Master Shan-tao, annotated translation by Zuio Hisao Inagaki, edited by Doyi Tan, Singapore, 2009, p.41-42
[137] *Idem*, p.45
[138] *Idem*, p.78

Vow, in harmony with the teaching, and in agreement with the Buddha's words".[139]

Master Shan-tao as quoted by Shinran Shonin in his *Kyogyoshinsho*

*

"Being mindful of Him (Amida Buddha) always, we board the Vow Power. After death we attain birth in His land, where we meet Him, face to face, with unbounded joy."

Master Shan-tao, *Ojoraisan*

*

"Let us realize, therefore, that when one comes to the hour of death, even though it be in a grass hut, at that very moment one can take his place upon the lotus seat. One can follow after Amida Nyorai and in company with a host of Bodhisattvas be born in a moment into the realm of the Pure Land which lies in the West ten thousand hundred millions lands away."[140]

Master Genshin, *Ojoyoshu*

*

*"Without regard for time, place, and various karmic relationships, merely reciting nembutsu makes birth in the Pure Land possible if one desires birth in the Pure Land at **the end of this life**".[141]*

---

[139] *Kyogyoshinsho – On Teaching, Practice, Faith, and Enlightenment*, translated by Hisao Inagaki, Numata Center for Buddhist Translation and Research, Kyoto, 2003, p. 34.

[140] *Genshin's Ojoyoshu – Collected Essays on Birth into the Pure Land*, translated from Japanese by A.K. Reischauer, The Transactions of the Asiatic Society of Japan, second series, volume VII, 1930, free online edition at http://www.amida-ji-retreat-temple-romania.blogspot.ro/2014/03/genshins-ojoyoshu-free-english-edition.html#more

[141] *The Promise of Amida Buddha: Honen's Path to Bliss* – the first English translation of the Genko edition of the works of Honen Shonin composed in Japanese - also known as *Collected Teachings of Kurodani Shonin: The Japanese*

Master Genshin as quoted by Honen Shonin in his *Admonitions for Attaining of Birth in the Pure Land*

*

"There is no discrepancy between either the words or the deeds of the many Buddhas. If Shakyamuni encouraged all ordinary people wholeheartedly and exclusively to engage in the one practice of the nembutsu while in their present bodies, and if He assured them that, after their lives had ended, they would surely be born in that land, then all the Buddhas of the ten directions will equally praise, equally encourage, and equally confirm this".[142]
Honen Shonin, *Senchakushu*

*

"Following the path of the Vow's Power, after death they can attain birth in that land [Amida's Land], where they will meet the Buddha and where their joy will know no end".[143]
Honen Shonin, *Senchakushu*

*

"When they lay aside their present lives, they will enter into the dwelling of the Buddhas, the Pure Land".[144]
Honen Shonin, *Senchakushu*

*

Anthology (Wago Toroku), translated by Joji Atone and Yoko Hayashi, Wisdom Publications, Boston, 2011, p. 400-401
[142] *Honen's Senchakushu – Passages on the Selection of the Nembutsu in the Original Vow (Senchaku Hongan Nembutsu Shu)*, translated and edited by Senchakushu English Translation Project, Kuroda Institute, University of Hawai'i Press, Honolulu and Sogo Bukkyo Kenkujo, Taisho University, Tokyo, p.104
[143] *Idem* p.110
[144] *Honen's Senchakushu – Passages on the Selection of the Nembutsu in the Original Vow (Senchaku Hongan Nembutsu Shu)*, translated and edited by Senchakushu English Translation Project, Kuroda Institute, University of Hawai'i Press, Honolulu and Sogo Bukkyo Kenkujo, Taisho University, Tokyo, p.121

"The nembutsu practitioners, after they have laid aside their present life, will certainly be born in the Land of Sukhavati".[145]

Honen Shonin, *Senchakushu*

*

"Master Shan-tao said that those whose faith in birth in the Pure Land in the next life and in the Primal Vow was less than profound would not enjoy the embrace and protection of holy beings. While reciting nembutsu, we must arouse profound faith, loathe this defiled world of suffering, and long for the Pure Land".[146]

Honen Shonin, *Wago Toroku*

*

"Question: 'How would it be to put your afterlife in the hands of a god'?

Answer: 'Nothing surpasses placing your future in the hands of Amida Buddha'".[147]

Honen Shonin, *Dialogue on One Hundred Forty-Five Topics*

*

"Foremost in the Pure Land of Ultimate Bliss, when I attain my birth,

will be the precious memory of fellow practitioners I left on earth".[148]

Honen Shonin, poems

---

[145] *Idem*, p.124

[146] *The Promise of Amida Buddha: Honen's Path to Bliss* – the first English translation of the Genko edition of the works of Honen Shonin composed in Japanese - also known as *Collected Teachings of Kurodani Shonin: The Japanese Anthology (Wago Toroku)*, translated by Joji Atone and Yoko Hayashi, Wisdom Publications, Boston, 2011, p. 174

[147] *Idem*, p. 284

[148] *Idem*, p. 319

*

"Recite nembutsu while wishing for deliverance and birth in the Pure Land in the life to come."[149]
Honen Shonin, *Replies to Saburo in Tsunoto*

*

"To pray for a good fortune in this ephemeral world and forgetting crucial deliverance in the next life are not the true meaning for nembutsu devotees. Amida Buddha designed nembutsu as the 'rightly established practice' for birth in the Pure Land in the life to come."[150]
Honen Shonin, *Wago Toroku*

*

"Regarding the life to come, one should not aspire for birth in a pure Buddha-land other than the Pure Land of Amida Buddha, nor should one hope to be born in the Tusita Heaven of Buddha Maitreya, nor desire to be reborn in the delusive worlds of human beings or heavenly beings".[151]
Honen Shonin, *Wago Toroku*

*

"Nothing but nembutsu will allow one to attain birth in the Pure Land in the life to come. I am not telling you this by my own initiative. I just state exactly what the sacred scriptures describe, as if holding the text up to a mirror. Please, look over the scriptures."[152]

---

[149] Idem p. 352
[150] *The Promise of Amida Buddha: Honen's Path to Bliss* – the first English translation of the Genko edition of the works of Honen Shonin composed in Japanese - also known as *Collected Teachings of Kurodani Shonin: The Japanese Anthology (Wago Toroku)*, translated by Joji Atone and Yoko Hayashi, Wisdom Publications, Boston, 2011, p. 365
[151] *Idem* p. 383
[152] *Idem*, p. 386

Honen Shonin, *Wago Toroku*

*

"Concerning 'the supreme working to embrace beings,' one of the Forty-eight Vows in the Larger Sutra says, 'If, when I become a Buddha, the sentient beings of the ten directions who, aspiring to be born in my land, call my Name even ten times, fail to be born there through my Vow-Power, may I not attain perfect Enlightenment.'

This means that the practitioners who aspire for birth are embraced by the Vow Power – when their lives are about to end – and are enabled to attain Birth. Hence, this is called "the supreme working to embrace beings."[153]

Shinran Shonin, *Kyogyoshinsho*

*

Shakyamuni urges all ordinary beings to practice the Nembutsu singleheartedly throughout their lives; **when they die, they will definitely be born in that land.** *All the Buddhas of the ten directions, without exception, praise and recommend this teaching and give testimony to its truth. Why do they do so? Because their great compassion arises from the same essence. One Buddha's teaching is the teaching of all the Buddhas; all the Buddhas' teachings are one Buddha's teaching.*[154]

The Master of Kuang-ming Temple says:

[...] the moment your life ends you will in the next moment be born in that land, where you will enjoy the Dharma pleasure of non-action for eternally long kalpas.[155]

Shinran Shonin, *Kyogyoshinsho*, chapter III

*

---

[153] *Kyogyoshinsho – On Teaching, Practice, Faith, and Enlightenment*, translated by Hisao Inagaki, Numata Center for Buddhist Translation and Research, Kyoto, 2003, p. 39.
[154] *Idem* p. 92.
[155] *Idem*, p. 125.

At the end of your life you will enter the family of the Buddhas, that is, the Pure Land.[156]

Shinran Shonin, *Kyogyoshinsho*, chapter III

*

Out of the thousands of people who received his teaching, personally or otherwise, over many days and years, very few were allowed to read and copy this book. Nevertheless, I was allowed to copy it and also make a copy of Genku's (Honen) portrait. This is the benefit of the exclusive practice of the act of right assurance; this is a sure proof of my future attainment of birth.[157]

Shinran Shonin, *Kyogyoshinsho*, chapter III

Here *"future attainment of birth"* clearly indicates birth in the Pure Land after death.

*

It is stated in the Collection of Passages on the Land of Peace and Bliss:
I have collected true words so that they may help others practice the way for Birth. For my wish is that those who have attained Birth may lead those who come after them and those who aspire for Birth may follow their predecessors, thus following one after another endlessly and uninterruptedly until the boundless sea of birth and death is exhausted.[158]

Shinran Shonin, *Kyogyoshinsho*, chapter IV

*

"Concerning the expression, 'Each living thing being grasped by Amida, a manifestation of the decisive cause of Birth': it is declared

---

[156] *Idem* p. 132.
[157] *Idem* p. 338.
[158] *Ibid.*

among the Forty-eight Vows taught in the Larger Sutra of Immeasurable Life:

'If, when I attain Buddhahood, the sentient beings of the ten quarters, aspiring to be born in my land, saying my Name even down to ten times, and being carried by the power of my Vow, were not to be born there, then may I not attain perfect Enlightenment.'
This means that practicers who aspire to be born are grasped by the power of the Vow and brought to attainment of Birth when their lives end. Hence the expression, 'Each living thing being grasped by Amida, a manifestation of the decisive cause of Birth'".[159]
Shinran Shonin, *Notes on the Inscriptions on Sacred Scrolls*

*

"...'Were not to be born there, then may I not attain perfect Enlightenment':
If people who entrust themselves to the Vow are not born in the true land fulfilled by the Primal Vow, I shall not become a Buddha.

This means that practicers who aspire to be born are grasped by the power of the Vow and brought to attainment of Birth when their lives end".[160]
Shinran Shonin, *Notes on the Inscriptions on Sacred Scrolls*

*

"I, for my own part, attach no significance to the condition, good or bad, of persons in their final moments. People in whom shinjin is determined do not doubt, and so abide among the truly settled. For this reason their end also – even for those ignorant and foolish and lacking in wisdom – is a happy one."[161]
Shinran Shonin, *Lamp for the Latter Ages*, Letter 6

---

[159] *The Collected Works of Shinran*, Shin Buddhism Translation Series, Jodo Shinshu Hongwanji-ha, Kyoto, 1997, p.505.
[160] *Idem* p. 06.
[161] *Idem* p.531.

*

"My life has now reached the fullness of years. It is certain that I will go to birth in the Pure Land before you, so without fail I will await you there".[162]

Shinran Shonin, *Lamp for the Latter Ages*, Letter 12

This clearly shows that Shinran Shonin associates his death with birth in the Pure Land.

*

"Since they dwell in the stage of non-retrogression until being born into the Pure Land, they are said to be in the stage of the truly settled.

Since true shinjin is awakened through the working of the two Honored Ones, Shakyamuni and Amida, it is when one is grasped that the settling of shinjin occurs. Thereafter the person abides in the stage of the truly settled until born into the Pure Land."[163]

Shinran Shonin, *Lamp for the Latter Ages*, Letter 13

So, as we see, entering the stage of non-retrogression when shinjin occurs in one's heart is not the same thing with being born into the Pure Land. As the passages clearly states, this stage is prior to birth there – *"until born into the Pure Land"*.

*

Kyoshin wrote a letter to Shinran in which he said:

"Those who attain true and real shinjin
Immediately join the truly settled;
Thus having entered the stage of non retrogression,
They necessarily attain Nirvana.

---

[162] *Idem.* 539.
[163] *Idem* p. 540.

The statement, 'they attain Nirvana', means that when the heart of the persons of true and real shinjin attain the fulfilled land at the end of his or her present life, that person becomes one with the light that is the heart of the Tathagata."[164]

Shinran Shonin, *Lamp for the Latter Ages*, Letter 14

Ren'i, another disciple, sent to him the answer of Shinran in which it was confirmed that the above statement was free from error:

"I conveyed the contents of your letter in detail to the Shonin, and he stated that it was altogether free from error."[165]

*

"The fulfillment of Myoho-bo's cherished desire to be born in the Pure Land is surely celebrated by those in Hitachi province who share the same aspiration."[166]

Shinran Shonin, *Lamp for the Latter Ages*, Letter 19

Here Shinran speaks about Myoho-bo's death which he equates with birth in the Pure Land.

*

"Please read the copies of Seikaku's Essentials of Faith Alone, Ryukan's On Self-power and Other-Power, and the other tracts I sent earlier. Such men are the best teachers for our times. Since they have already been born in the Pure Land, nothing can surpass what is written in their tracts. They understood Master Honen's teaching fully and for this reason attained perfect Birth."[167]

Shinran Shonin, *Lamp for the Latter Ages*, Letter 19

---

[164] *Idem* 541.

[165] *Idem* p. 543.

[166] *Idem* p. 550.

[167] *Ibid*

At the moment Shinran wrote this letter, Master Seikaku and Master Ryukan were dead, so their birth in the Pure Land was attained in their after life.

*

While criticizing some disciples, Shinran said, *"Such people have no aspiration for the nembutsu nor for the Buddha's Vow; thus, however diligently they engage in the nembutsu with such an attitude, it is difficult for them to attain Birth in the next life."*[168]
Shinran Shonin, *Lamp for the Latter Ages*, Letter 19

*

" I am truly sad to hear about Kakunen-bo. I had expected that I would go first to the Pure Land, but I have been left behind; it is unutterably saddening. Kakushin-bo, who left us last year, has certainly gone to the Pure Land and is awaiting us there. Needless to say, I will surely meet them there; it is beyond words. Kakunen-bo's words did not differ at all from what I have said, so we will certainly go to the same place, the Pure Land. If I am still alive in the tenth month of next year, it will undoubtedly be possible to meet again in this world. Since your mind of entrusting also does not differ at all from my own, even if I go first, I will await you in the Pure Land"[169]
Shinran Shonin, *Uncollected Letters*, Letter 2

Here again, Shinran equates the death of one of his disciples (Kakunen-bo) with birth in the Pure Land.

*

"Further, having no thought of wanting to go to the Pure Land quickly, we think forlornly that we may die even when we become slightly ill; this is the action of blind passions. It is hard for us to abandon this old home of pain, where we have been transmigrating

---

[168] *Idem* p. 551.
[169] *Idem* p. 579 - 580.

111

for innumerable kalpas down to the present, and we feel no longing for the Pure Land of peace, where we have yet to be born. Truly, how powerful our blind passions are! But though we feel reluctant to part from this world, at the moment our karmic bonds to this saha world run out and helplessly we die, we shall go to that land."[170]

Shinran Shonin, *Tannisho,* chapter 9

*

"The point is to keep the matter of Other Power faith firmly in mind. Beyond that, you should just say the nembutsu—walking, standing, sitting, and lying down—in gratitude for Amida Buddha's benevolence. With this understanding, the birth that is to come in the Pure Land is assured".[171]

Rennyo Shonin, *Letters*

"Birth that is to come in the Pure Land" clearly means not "here and now" in this life, as we'll see from the next passages.

*

"I don't know why, but recently (this summer), I have been particularly subject to drowsiness, and when I consider why I should be so lethargic, I feel without a doubt that the moment of death leading to birth in the Pure Land may be close at hand."[172]

Rennyo Shonin, *Letters*

*

"Those who become wives of the priests in charge of lodgings on this mountain at Yoshizaki should be aware that this happens because past conditions in their previous lives are not shallow. This awareness, however, will come about after they have realized that the

---

[170] *Idem*, p. 666.

[171] *Rennyo Shonin Ofumi: The Letters of Rennyo*, translated from the Japanese (Taisho, Volume 74, Number 2668) by Ann T. Rogers and Minor L. Rogers, Numata Center for Buddhist Translation and Research, Berkeley, California, 1996, p.16

[172] *Idem* p.17

afterlife is the matter of greatest importance and undergone a decisive settling of faith. Therefore those who are to be wives of the priests should, by all means, firmly attain faith.

First of all, because what is known as settled mind in our tradition differs greatly from and is superior to [the understanding of] the Jodo schools in general, it is said to be the great faith of Other Power. Therefore, we should realize that those who have attained this faith—ten out of ten, one hundred out of one hundred—are assured of the birth that is to come in the Pure Land."[173]

Rennyo Shonin, *Letters*

*

"If you wish to attain faith and entrust yourselves to Amida, first realize that human life endures only as long as a dream or an illusion and that the afterlife in the Pure Land is indeed the blissful result in eternity, that human life means the enjoyment of only fifty to a hundred years, and that the afterlife is the matter of greatest importance."[174]

Rennyo Shonin, *Letters*

*

*"Let us realize, then, that what we should earnestly aspire to is **birth in the Pure Land in the afterlife**, that the one we should rely upon is Amida Tathagata, and that the place to which we go after faith is decisively settled is the Pure Land of serene sustenance. These days, however, the priests in this region who are nembutsu people are seriously at variance with the Buddha-Dharma. That is, they call followers from whom they receive donations 'good disciples' and speak of them as 'people of faith.' This is a serious error. Also, the disciples think that if they just bring an abundance of things to the priests, they will be saved by the priests' power, even if their own power is insufficient. This, too, is an error. And so between*

---

[173] *Idem*, p.22
[174] *Idem* p.23

the priests and their followers, there is not a modicum of understanding of our tradition's faith. This is indeed deplorable. Without a doubt, neither priests nor disciples will be born in the Land of Utmost Bliss; they will fall in vain into hell.

Even though we lament this, we cannot lament deeply enough; though we grieve, we should grieve more deeply. From now on, therefore, the priests should seek out those who fully know the details of the great faith of Other Power, let their faith be decisively settled, and then teach the essentials of that faith to their disciples; together, they will surely attain **the birth that is to come** in the Pure Land, which is the most important matter."[175]

Rennyo Shonin, *Letters*

*

"What is fundamental is that we simply discard the sundry practices and take refuge in the right practice. To take refuge in the right practice is just to rely on Amida Tathagata singleheartedly and steadfastly, without any contriving. Sentient beings everywhere who entrust themselves in this way are embraced within Amida's light; He does not abandon them, and **when life is spent**, He brings them without fail to the Pure Land. It is through this single minded faith alone that we are born in the Pure Land. How readily we attain this settled mind—there is no effort on our part! Hence the two characters 'anjin' are read 'easily attained mind'; they have this meaning."[176]

Rennyo Shonin, *Letters*

*

"We should realize that we have been received within Amida Tathagata's all-pervading light and that we will dwell within this light for the duration of our lives. Then, when life is spent, Amida brings us at once to the true and real fulfilled land."[177]

---

[175] *Idem* p.24
[176] *Idem*, p.43
[177] *Idem* p.46

114

Rennyo Shonin, *Letters*

*

"Then, in order to be saved in regard to the most important matter, **the afterlife,** *how do we entrust ourselves to Amida Tathagata? The answer is that when we entrust ourselves without any worry or double-mindedness - casting away all sundry practices and miscellaneous good acts and relying on Amida Tathagata singleheartedly and steadfastly - Amida sends forth His light and embraces within it the sentient beings who rely on Him. This is called 'receiving the benefit of Amida Tathagata's embracing light.' It is also called 'receiving the benefit of the Vow that never abandons us.' Once we have been received in this way within Amida Tathagata's light, we will be born immediately into the true and real fulfilled land when life is spent. Let there be no doubt about this."*[178]

Rennyo Shonin, *Letters*

*

"In this province and others, there are many these days who are sharply at variance with what our tradition teaches about the settled mind. Each person feels that he understands correctly, and few think of making further effort to attain true and real faith by asking others about views that run counter to the Dharma. This is indeed a deplorable attachment. Unless **the birth that is to come** *in the fulfilled land is decisively settled by their quickly repenting and confessing these views and abiding in our tradition's true and real faith, it is indeed just as if they went to a mountain of treasure and returned empty- handed."*[179]

Rennyo Shonin, *Letters*

*

---

[178] *Idem* p.60-61
[179] *Idem,* p.67

115

*"Those who intend to come without fail on the twenty-eighth of every month must understand that people in whom the settled mind is yet to be realized (mianjin) and for whom the customary ways of faith are not decisively established should, by all means, quickly attain Other Power faith based on the truth and reality of the Primal Vow, thereby decisively settling **the birth that is to come** in the fulfilled land. It is this that will truly accomplish their own resolve to repay their indebtedness and express their gratitude for the Master's benevolence. This also means that, as a matter of course, their objective of birth in the Land of Utmost Bliss is assured. It is, in other words, entirely consistent with what is expressed in Shan-tao's commentary:*

'To realize faith oneself and to guide others to faith is the most difficult of all difficulties; to tell of great Compassion and awaken beings everywhere is truly to respond in gratitude to the Buddha's benevolence.'"[180]

Rennyo Shonin, *Letters*

*

"Therefore, given this present occasion, if there are people who have not realized the faith that is the truth and reality of the Primal Vow, we must indeed conclude they have not received the prompting of good from the past. If there were not people for whom good from the past had unfolded, all would be in vain and the birth that is to come in the Pure Land could not be settled. This would be the one thing to be lamented above all else."[181]

Rennyo Shonin, *Letters*

*

"What we should bear in mind is that it is indeed through Amida Tathagata's gracious and vast benevolence that birth in the Pure Land is settled; and with this realization, sleeping or waking, we

---

[180] *Idem*, p.69
[181] *Idem*, p.70

116

simply say 'Namo Amida Butsu' in gratitude for the Buddha's benevolence.

What else, then, do we need besides this for **birth in the afterlife**? Is it not truly deplorable that some people confuse others by talking about false teachings that are of uncertain origin and are unknown to us, and furthermore that they debase the transmission of the Dharma? You must reflect on this very carefully."[182]

Rennyo Shonin, *Letters*

*

"Having thus attained the faith that is expressed through the nembutsu, we should then realize that, although we are wretched beings of deep evil karma who commit evil all our lives, when we once awaken faith with the one thought-moment of taking refuge in Amida, we are readily saved by the working of the Buddha's Vow. Then, deeply recognizing the graciousness of Amida Tathagata's inconceivable, all-surpassing Primal Vow – the strong cause of Birth - we simply say the nembutsu, sleeping or waking, in gratitude for the Buddha's benevolence, and repay our indebtedness to Amida Tathagata.

Nothing we know beyond this is of any use for **the attainment of birth in the afterlife**, but these days, people talk absurdly - as if something were lacking - about unknown, eccentric teachings that have not been transmitted within our tradition; thus they confuse others and debase the unsurpassed transmission of the Dharma. This is indeed a deplorable situation. We must think about it very carefully."[183]

Rennyo Shonin, *Letters*

Especially in our days, when various false teachings are given more and more space in the international sangha, we must reflect deeply on the above warnings of Rennyo Shonin.

*

---

[182] *Idem*, p.73
[183] *Idem*, p.78-79

117

"We find, therefore, that if people who seek birth through the nembutsu do not realize faith through the prompting of past causes, the birth to come in the fulfilled land is impossible. In the words of the Master, the point of this is: 'If you should realize faith, rejoice in conditions from the distant past'."[184]

Rennyo Shonin, *Letters*

*

"The way of the world is, above all, that we continue on as if unaware of the uncertainty of life for young and old alike. Existence is as ephemeral as a flash of lightning or the morning dew, and the wind of impermanence may come even now. Yet we think only of prolonging this life for as long as possible, without ever aspiring to **birth in the Pure Land in the afterlife.** *This is inexpressibly deplorable.*

From today, we should quickly entrust ourselves to Amida Tathagata's Primal Vow of Other Power. Steadfastly taking refuge in the Buddha of Immeasurable Life, we should aspire to birth in the true and real fulfilled land and repeat the nembutsu, saying the Name of the Buddha."[185]

Rennyo Shonin, *Letters*

*

"When we simply take refuge in this Primal Vow with sincere mind, with the awakening of the one thought-moment in which there is no doubt, then, without any anxiety, birth in the Pure Land is assured if we die at that time. Or, if life is prolonged, then during that time, we should say the nembutsu in gratitude for the Buddha's benevolence and await our lives' end."[186]

Rennyo Shonin, *Letters*

---

[184] *Idem*, p.82
[185] *Idem*, p.84
[186] *Idem*, p.87

*

*"The meaning of our tradition's settled mind is that, regardless of the depth of our own evil hindrances, there is no doubt whatsoever that Amida will save all sentient beings who simply put a stop to their inclination toward the sundry practices, single heartedly take refuge in Amida Tathagata, and deeply entrust themselves to Him to save them in regard to the most important Matter – the **birth that is to come in the afterlife**. Those who thoroughly understand in this way will indeed be born in the Pure Land, one hundred out of one hundred."*[187]

Rennyo Shonin, *Letters*

*

"Considering that the human realm is a place of uncertainty for young and old alike, we will surely undergo some sort of illness and die. Everyone must understand that, given the circumstances in a world like this, it is essential that faith be settled decisively and promptly - indeed, as soon as possible - and that we be assured of the birth to come in the Land of Utmost Bliss."[188]

Rennyo Shonin, *Letters*

*

"When we abandon the sundry practices and steadfastly and single heartedly rely on Amida to save us in regard to the afterlife, there is no doubt at all that we will be born without fail in the Land of Utmost Bliss."[189]

Rennyo Shonin, *Letters*

*

---

[187] *Idem*, p.101
[188] *Idem*, p.102
[189] *Idem*, p.104

"It has been said that those who do not know the importance of the afterlife are foolish, even though they may understand eighty thousand sutras and teachings; those who know about the afterlife are wise, even though they may be unlettered men and women."[190]

Rennyo Shonin, *Letters*

*

"As the Master [Shinran] has said, no men or women will ever be saved without entrusting themselves to Amida's Primal Vow. Hence there should be no doubt at all that those who abandon the sundry practices and, with the awakening of the one thought-moment, deeply entrust themselves to Amida Tathagata to save them in regard to the afterlife will all be born in Amida's fulfilled land, whether ten people or one hundred - whatever sort of men or women they may be."[191]

Rennyo Shonin, *Letters*

*

"Women who rely firmly and without any anxiety on Amida Tathagata and accept that Amida saves them in regard to the most important matter, the afterlife, will unfailingly be saved. If, leaving the depth of their evil to Amida, they simply rely single heartedly on Amida Tathagata to save them in regard to the afterlife, there is no doubt that Amida, fully knowing those beings, will save them."[192]

Rennyo Shonin, *Letters*

*

"Because the impermanence of this world creates a condition of uncertainty for young and old alike, we should all immediately take

---

[190] *Idem*, p.107
[191] *Idem*, p.108
[192] *Idem*, p.118-119

to heart the most important matter, the afterlife, and, deeply entrusting ourselves to Amida Buddha, and say the nembutsu."[193]

Rennyo Shonin, *Letters*

---

[193] *Idem*, p.118-119

2) Passages which show that birth in the Pure Land takes place after death and it means the attainment of Nirvana (Enlightenment/Buddhahood)

"However hard you may practice in this life, it can only be for a short while. In the life to come you will be born in the land of Amitayus (Amida) and enjoy endless bliss there. Being forever in accord with the Way, you will no longer be subject to birth and death and be free of the afflictions caused by greed, anger and ignorance."[194]

Shakyamuni Buddha, *The Larger Sutra*

*

*"If sentient beings in the three realms of suffering see His (Amida's) light they will all be relieved and freed from affliction. **At the end of their lives, they all reach liberation.**"*[195]

The Larger Sutra as quoted by Shinran Shonin in his Kyogyoshinsho, chapter V

Here to *"see the Light"* means to receive faith in Amida Buddha.

*

"If at the end of life one obtains birth into this country (the Pure Land) then one has boundless virtues. I, therefore, do nothing but offer my life to Amida and desire to enter the Pure Land."[196]

---

[194] *The Three Pure Land Sutras*, translated by Hisao Inagaki in collaboration with Harold Stewart, revised second edition, Numata Center for Buddhist Translation and Research, Berkeley, California, 2003, p. 53

[195] *Kyogyoshinsho – On Teaching, Practice, Faith, and Enlightenment*, translated by Hisao Inagaki, Numata Center for Buddhist Translation and Research, Kyoto, 2003, p. 198.

[196] *Genshin's Ojoyoshu – Collected Essays on Birth into the Pure Land*, translated from Japanese by A.K. Reischauer, The Transactions of the Asiatic Society of Japan, second series, volume VII, 1930, free online edition at http://www.amida-ji-retreat-temple-romania.blogspot.ro/2014/03/genshins-ojoyoshu-free-english-edition.html#more

Bodhisattva Nagarjuna as quoted by Master Genshin in his *Ojoyoshu*

*

*"Sentient beings who practice the nembutsu are embraced by Amida Buddha and never abandoned; **at the end of their lives** they will certainly be born in the Pure Land."*[197]

Master Tao-ch'o as quoted by Honen Shonin in his *Senchakushu*

*

"If sentient beings in the three realms of suffering see His Light, they will all be relieved and freed from affliction. At the end of their lives, they all reach emancipation". [198]

Master Shan-tao, *Ojoraisan*

*

*"Generally speaking, the nembutsu practitioner is extolled with the five epithets and is blessed with the close protection of the two Honored Ones (Avalokitesvara and Mahasthamaprapta). These are the present benefits. **The future benefit** is that the practitioner will be born in the Pure Land and will eventually become a Buddha".*[199]

Honen Shonin, *Senchakushu*

*

---

[197] *Honen's Senchakushu – Passages on the Selection of the Nembutsu in the Original Vow (Senchaku Hongan Nembutsu Shu)*, translated and edited by Senchakushu English Translation Project, Kuroda Institute, University of Hawai'i Press, Honolulu and Sogo Bukkyo Kenkujo, Taisho University, Tokyo, p.124

[198] *Shan-tao's Liturgy for Birth – Ojoraisan*, compiled by Master Shan-tao, annotated translation by Zuio Hisao Inagaki, edited by Doyi Tan, Singapore, 2009, p.46

[199] *Honen's Senchakushu – Passages on the Selection of the Nembutsu in the Original Vow (Senchaku Hongan Nembutsu Shu)*, translated and edited by Senchakushu English Translation Project, Kuroda Institute, University of Hawai'i Press, Honolulu and Sogo Bukkyo Kenkujo, Taisho University, Tokyo, p.124

*"Generally speaking, the nembutsu practitioner is extolled with the five epithets and is blessed with the close protection of the two Honored Ones (Avalokitesvara and Mahasthamaprapta). These are the present benefits. **The future benefit** is that the practitioner will be born in the Pure Land and will eventually become a Buddha".*[200]

Honen Shonin, *Senchakushu*

*

"We read in the commentary of the Master of Kuang-ming Temple: '[...]We should sincerely devote ourselves to this teaching until the end of our life and, after abandoning our defiled bodies, realize the eternal bliss of Dharma-nature[201] *,"*[202]

Shinran Shonin, *Kyogyoshinsho*, chapter IV

*

---

[200] *Ibid.*

[201] Samsaric or unenlightened beings are like seeds dropped in an infertile soil. Although the potentiality of any seed is to become a tree, if you place it in a poor soil, devoid of any good nutrients, and in the presence of various bad weeds, the seed will not grow.

Just like the seed, the potentiality of any being is to become a Buddha (this is what is meant by all beings have Buddha-nature), but because we live in this samsaric world, itself the effect and echo of our own evil karma, we cannot grow and transform ourselves into Buddhas.

This is exactly why we need to let Amida take us to His Pure Land. That Land is the best soil for seeds like us to quickly develop their natural potential and become Buddhas. Unlike the various Samsaric planes of existence, the Pure Land is the soil (realm) of Enlightenment, the perfect garden manifested by Amida Buddha where everything is conducive to Enlightenment. So, we should all simply entrust to Him and wish to be planted/reborn there, where by receiving all the necesary nutrients and not being obstructed by any bad weeds, we'll naturally transform ourselves into Trees of Enlightenment.

[202] *Kyogyoshinsho – On Teaching, Practice, Faith, and Enlightenment*, translated by Hisao Inagaki, Numata Center for Buddhist Translation and Research, Kyoto, 2003, p. 175.

"Whether one is left behind or goes before, it is surely a sorrowful thing to be parted by death. But the one who first attains Nirvana vows without fail to save those who where close to him first and leads those with whom he has been karmically bound, his relatives, and his friends."[203]

Shinran Shonin, *Lamp for the Latter Ages*, Letter 14

*

"As for me, Shinran, I have never said the nembutsu even once for the repose of my departed father and mother. For all sentient beings, without exception, have been our parents and brothers and sisters in the course of countless lives in the many states of existence. On attaining Buddhahood after this present life, we can save every one of them."[204]

Shinran Shonin, *Tannisho*, chapter 5

*

"By virtue of being shone upon by Amida's light, we receive diamond like shinjin when the one thought-moment of entrusting arises within us; hence, already in that instant Amida takes us into the stage of the truly settled, and when our lives end, all our blind passions and obstructions of evil being transformed, we are brought to realize insight into the non-origination of all existence".[205]

Shinran Shonin, *Tannisho*, chapter 14

*

"If we entrust ourselves to Amida's Vow that grasps and never abandons us, then even though unforeseen circumstances, we commit an evil act and die without saying the nembutsu at the very end, we will immediately realize birth in the Pure Land.

---

[203] *The Collected Works of Shinran*, Shin Buddhism Translation Series, Jodo Shinshu Hongwanji-ha, Kyoto, 1997, p. 545.
[204] *Idem*, p. 664.
[205] *Idem*, p. 673.

Moreover, even if we do say the Name at the point of death, it will be nothing other than our expression of gratitude for Amida's benevolence, entrusting ourselves to the Buddha more and more as the very time of Enlightenment draws near."[206]

Shinran Shonin, *Tannisho*, chapter 14

*

"Do those who speak of realizing Enlightenment while in this bodily existence manifest various accommodated bodies, possess the Buddha's thirty-two features and eighty marks, and preach the Dharma to benefit beings like Shakyamuni? It is this that is meant by realizing Enlightenment in this life.

It is stated in a hymn:

When the time comes
For shinjin, indestructible as diamond, to become settled,
Amida grasps and protects us with compassion and light,
So that we may part forever from birth-and-death.

*This means that at the moment shinjin becomes settled, we are grasped, never to be abandoned, and therefore we will not transmigrate further in the six courses. Only then do we part forever from birth-and-death. **Should such awareness be confusedly termed "attaining Enlightenment"**? It is regrettable that such misunderstanding should arise.*

*The late Master said, according to the true essence of the Pure Land way, **one entrusts oneself to the Primal Vow in this life and realizes Enlightenment in the Pure Land**; this is the teaching I received."[207]*

Shinran Shonin, *Tannisho*, chapter 15

Birth in the Pure Land and Enlightenment are attained only after death. Shinjin or entrusting to Amida Buddha's Primal Vow, which is

---

[206] *Idem*, p. 673-674.
[207] *Idem*, p. 675.

received in this life and makes us enter in the stage of those assured of birth in the Pure Land, must not be confused with the actual attainment of birth in the Pure Land. Hence, the true teaching is, *"one entrusts oneself to the Primal Vow in this life and realizes Enlightenment in the Pure Land[208]"*.

---

[208] **Question:** What part of our mind goes to the Pure Land? Is it the mind we currently have, in others words is it who we are now that goes to be born in the Pure Land?"

Answer: What we know for sure is that birth in the Pure Land takes place after physical death. This is what the Masters of our tradition clearly said, so we accept it.

At death, what we call 'mind stream' leaves the physical body and instead of passing through bardo (intermediary state) and then to other states of existence, it goes directly to the Pure Land where Enlightenment happens immediately. At that very moment, the delusions of our 'mind stream' are naturally melt like ice meeting fire, and our true enlightened nature will appear. So, we may say that we go to the Pure Land as we are, but once born there, in the safe and enlightened realm of Amida, 'we' transform into something completely different, that is, fully Enlightened Buddhas.

But all these things are inconceivable and beyond conceptual understanding, so I cannot enter into further analysis. Some aspects are impossible to understand at the level we are now as unenlightened beings. Now all we need to do is to simply entrust to Amida. Jodo Shinshu is the path of simple faith, not of profound understanding in this life of the ultimate nature of mind.

3) Passages which show the enlightened qualities of those born in the Pure Land of Amida, and which can't be found in the "here and now" samsaric bodies and minds of unenlightened followers.

I have always wondered how can one say that the "Pure Land is here and now" or in "the mind" if he cannot actually manifest, here and now, the qualities of the Pure Land? Indeed, how can one be in the Pure Land, but continue to be impure in one's mind and still unenlightened? This is clear evidence that such views do not belong to the Dharma Gate of the Pure Land, or to the simple faith oriented teaching of Jodo Shinshu.

In the *Larger Sutra* it is said:
"They are of noble and majestic countenance, unequaled in all the worlds, and their appearance is superb, unmatched by any being, heavenly or human. They are all endowed with bodies of Naturalness, Emptiness, and Infinity."[209]

So, are those deluded scholars who claim that the Pure Land is "here and now" endowed with *"bodies of Naturalness, Emptiness, and Infinity"*? Shinran himself made reference to the same passage from the *Larger Sutra*, in his work *Passages on the Pure Land Way [REALIZATION]* :

"Their countenances are dignified and wonderful, surpassing things of this world. Their features, subtle and delicate, are not those of human beings or devas; all receive the body of naturalness or of emptiness, the body of boundlessness."[210]
Do they have the color of pure gold, as promised to those born in the Pure Land in the 3rd Vow?

---

[209] *The Three Pure Land Sutras*, translated by Hisao Inagaki in collaboration with Harold Stewart, revised second edition, Numata Center for Buddhist Translation and Research, Berkeley, California, 2003, p.31
[210] *The Collected Works of Shinran*, Shin Buddhism Translation Series, Jodo Shinshu Hongwanji-ha, Kyoto, 1997, p.300

128

"If, when I attain Buddhahood, humans and devas in my land[211] should not all be the color of pure gold, may I not attain perfect Enlightenment." (the 3rd Vow)

Do they have the same appearance, as promised in the 4th Vow?

"If, when I attain Buddhahood, humans and devas in my land should not all be of one appearance, and should there be any difference in beauty, may I not attain perfect Enlightenment." (the 4th Vow)

Unenlightened beings in samsara have various forms and shapes, color and beauty. They differ greatly from one another and this is due to the different types of karma they inherit from past lives. But once they are born in the Pure Land and become Buddhas they are liberated from the shackles of karma and go beyond form, color and any differences. This is what is meant by *"all be of one appearance"*. To be of the color of pure gold also means to have transcendent bodies of the qualities of Enlightenment. So, again, are those deluded scholars in this situation?

More than this, in the 21st Vow it is promised that beings in the Pure Land are *"endowed with the thirty-two physical characteristics*

---

[211] Beings born in the Pure Land are sometimes called *"humans and devas (gods) in my land"*, which doesn't mean that in the Pure Land there are the six unenlightened realms of existence, namely the hells, hungry spirits, animals, humans, fighting spirits (demigods) and gods. Shakyamuni himself explains in the *Larger Sutra* that when the expression *"humans and devas"* in the Pure Land appears in this sacred discourse it is only in relation with the states of existence prior to their birth in the Pure Land:

"They are all of one form, without any differences, but are called 'heavenly beings'(devas) and 'humans' simply by analogy with the states of existence in other worlds. They are of noble and majestic countenance, unequaled in all the worlds, and their appearance is superb, unmatched by any being, heavenly or human. They are all endowed with bodies of Naturalness, Emptiness, and Infinity."

For a detailed explanation of all the 48 Vows of Amida Buddha, see my book *The 48 Vows of Amida Buddha*, Dharma Lion Publications, Craiova. 2013

of a Great Man". Shakyamuni Buddha too, said the same in the *Larger Sutra* about those born in the Pure Land of Amida:

"Ananda, the sentient beings born there all fully posses the thirty two physical characteristics of a Great Man as well as perfect wisdom, with which they penetrate deeply into the nature of all dharmas and reach their subtle essence. Their supernatural powers know no obstruction and their physical senses are sharp and clear".

Clearly if we check their samsaric bodies no one claiming that the Pure Land is "here and now" have the *"thirty two physical characteristics of a Great Man".* But perhaps they have *"perfect wisdom, with which they penetrate deeply into the nature of all dharmas and reach their subtle essence"* or some kind of *"supernatural powers"* which they keep secret from us, ordinary guys with a simple faith?

Maybe they all have unlimited life-spans[212] (15th Vow), remember *"all their previous lives"* and know *"the events which occurred during the previous hundred thousand kotis of nayutas of kalpas"* (the 5th Vow) or they *"possess the divine eye of seeing even a hundred thousand kotis of nayutas of Buddha-lands"* (6th Vow), and *"the faculty of knowing the thoughts of others"* (the 8th Vow). They are probably *"endowed with the body of the Vajra-god Narayana"*[213]

---

[212] Those born in the Pure Land are beyond death, so their bodies of manifestations have unlimited life span.

[213] Vajra- god Narayana is in fact Vajrapani (from Sanskrit vajra, "thunderbolt" or "diamond" and pani, lit. "in the hand"), one of the most important Enlightened Bodhisattvas of Mahayana Buddhism. He is the protector of Buddha Dharma, and He represents the Power of all Buddhas. Just as Samantabhadra Bodhisattva, mentioned in the 22nd Vow, represents the endless saving activity of all Buddhas, Vajrapani represents the immense and all surpassing Power of the Buddhas. Those born in the Pure Land are exactly like these two Enlightened Bodhisattvas. Just like Samantabhadra they are always active in samsara, and like Vajrapani they are all-powerful. And because Vajrapani is a protector of the Dharma, beings in the Pure Land will forever protect it and destroy wrong understandings, which is clearly something those deluded scholars do not do "here and now", but actually destroy the Dharma with their personal views.

(26th Vow) or are able to go *"anywhere in one instant, even beyond a hundred thousand kotis of nayutas of Buddha-lands"* (9th Vow), have the *"divine ear of hearing the teachings of at least a hundred thousand kotis of nayutas of Buddhas"* and *"remember all of them"* (7th Vow), worship directly all Buddhas in all the ten directions (24th Vow) and make offerings to them (23rd Vow), *"hear spontaneously whatever teachings they may wish"* (the 46th Vow), etc.

Perhaps they never *"give rise to thoughts of self-attachment"* (10th Vow) and they are *"free of mental hindrances, pure in mind and without indolence."* Perhaps, as Shakyamuni said, *"their samsaric bodies and evil passions have been extinguished together with their remaining karmic tendencies"* [214]. Maybe *"their wisdom is like the ocean, and their Samadhi, like the king of mountains"*[215].....

The enlightened qualities of those born in the Pure Land are described in length in the *Larger Sutra*, so I invite anyone having the illusion that he or she is "here and now" in the Pure Land to carefully read those passages and reflect on them. Next, I'll show you more quotes from various Jodo Shinshu masters who themselves explained the Pure Land to be the realm where Enlightenment is attained.

"That Buddha-land is filled with innumerable means that lead us to take refuge,
And there are neither evil realms nor evil teachers.
One who is born there attains Enlightenment without fail.
Therefore, I pay homage to Amida Buddha, the most Honored One".[216]
Bodhisattva Nagarjuna, *Twelve Praises of Amida Buddha (Junirai)*

*

---

[214] *The Three Pure Land Sutras*, translated by Hisao Inagaki in collaboration with Harold Stewart, revised second edition, Numata Center for Buddhist Translation and Research, Berkeley, California, 2003, p.44
[215] Ibid.
[216] *The Pure Land Writings*, vol I, The Indian Masters, general editor Tokunaga Michio, The Shin Buddhism Translation Series, Jodo Shinshu Hongwanji-ha, Kyoto, 2012, p.42.

"The stature of the heavenly beings is as high as the top of Gold Mountain. Many beautiful scenes welcome their approach. Those who are born into this country can see with their heavenly eyes across the universe without restrictions. The saints bow to them in welcome. The beings in this country have miraculous powers and knowledge of their destiny. Therefore they depend upon Buddha for life and they worship him."[217]

Bodhisattva Nagarjuna as quoted by Master Genshin in his *Ojoyoshu*

*

"The land is filled with numerous kinds of fragrance.
Its pure sound[218] deeply enlightens beings far and wide.
Subtle and wondruous, it is heard throughout the ten quarters.
Amida, the perfectly Enlightened,
Who is its Dharma-king, fully sustains it.
The beings of this Tathagata's pure lotus
Are born transformed from the lotus of perfect Enlightenment.
Enjoying the taste of the Buddha Dharma,
They partake of meditation and Samadhi as their food.
Forever free from physical and mental afflictions,
They constantly enjoy pleasure without interruption.
In the world of good of the Mahayana, all beings are equal.
And not even the words of disparagement exist.
Now is anyone born there as
A woman, or disabled, or one having the seeds of two vehicles.
All that sentient beings desire
Are perfectly fulfilled in that land

---

[217] *Genshin's Ojoyoshu – Collected Essays on Birth into the Pure Land*, translated from Japanese by A.K. Reischauer, The Transactions of the Asiatic Society of Japan, second series, volume VII, 1930, free online edition at http://www.amida-ji-retreat-temple-romania.blogspot.ro/2014/03/genshins-ojoyoshu-free-english-edition.html#more

[218] According to Master T'an-luan's commentary, this indicated the name of Amida's Pure Land – cf. *The Pure Land Writings*, vol I, The Indian Masters, general editor Tokunaga Michio, The Shin Buddhism Translation Series, Jodo Shinshu Hongwanji-ha, Kyoto, 2012, fn 1, p.47

For this reason I aspire to be born
In the Buddha Land of Amida."[219]
Bodhisattva Vasubandhu, *Treatise on the Pure Land (Jodoron)*

*

"We should know that the reward of the Pure Land is free from the
defect of the two kinds of disparagement: one is the beings, and the
other is their names. The three kinds of beings who do not exist there
are: 1) those of the two vehicles, 2) women[220], and 3) the disabled.
Since these three kinds of people do not exist there, it is said to be
free of disparagement. There are also three kinds of disparaging
terms. Since the three kinds of beings do not exist, likewise even those
disparaging terms do not exist. Furthermore, three kinds of terms,
such as those of the two vehicles, women, and the disabled, are
unknown. This is why the land is said to be free of disparaging
words. 'Equal' means being equal in appearance."[221]
Bodhisattva Vasubandhu, *Treatise on the Pure Land (Jodoron)*

*

"The fifth gate in the phase of 'going out' is to observe with great
compassion all suffering beings, manifest accommodated and
transformed bodies, and enter
   the garden of birth and death and the forest of evil passions, where
[bodhisattvas] play about, exercising supernatural powers; they thus

---

[219] *The Pure Land Writings*, vol I, The Indian Masters, general editor Tokunaga Michio, The Shin Buddhism Translation Series, Jodo Shinshu Hongwanji-ha, Kyoto, 2012, p.47

[220] No women are to be found in the Pure Land in the sense that all beings born there go beyond womanhood and manhood, attaining supreme Enlightenment beyond any form or discrimination. See my explanation of the 35th Vow on the salvation of women from my book, *The 48 Vows of Amida Buddha*, Dharma Lion Publications, Craiova, 2013, p.51

[221] *The Pure Land Writings*, vol I, The Indian Masters, general editor Tokunaga Michio, The Shin Buddhism Translation Series, Jodo Shinshu Hongwanji-ha, Kyoto, 2012, p.56

dwell in the stage of teaching others through merit transference by [Amida's] Primal Vow-Power.'"[222]

Bodhisattva Vasubandhu as quoted by Shinran Shonin in his *Kyogyoshinsho*, chapter IV

*

"Upon attaining birth in the Pure Land, people feel neither enmity nor forbearance."[223]

Master T'an-luan, *Ojoronchu*

*

"Not even the names of the three realms of suffering are heard there, but only Nirvanic sounds of bliss. For this reason, that land is called 'Peace and Bliss'."[224]

Master T'an-luan, *Ojoronchu*

*

"The Pure Land is the realm which is shared by its pure inhabitants."[225]

Master T'an-luan, *Ojoronchu*

*

When ordinary human beings full of evil passions attain birth in the Pure Land, the karmic bonds of the three worlds will no longer

---

[222] *Kyogyoshinsho – On Teaching, Practice, Faith, and Enlightenment*, translated by Hisao Inagaki, Numata Center for Buddhist Translation and Research, Kyoto, 2003, p. 195.

[223] *Ojoronchu – T'an-luan's Commentary on Vasubandhu's Discourse on the Pure Land*, a study and translation by Hisao Inagaki, Nagata Bunshodo, Kyoto, 1998, p.222

[224] *Idem*, p.227-228

[225] *Idem*, p.268

affect them. Even without severing evil passions they will attain the state of Nirvana.[226]

Master T'an-luan as quoted by Shinran in his *Kyogyoshinsho*, chapter IV

*

"Question: To which of the three worlds does the Land of Peace and Bliss belong?

Answer: The Pure Land is supreme and excellent, its essential quality exceeding the worldly realms. The three worlds are the dark house of Samsara inhabited by ordinary people. Though there are different degrees of pleasure and pain and different lengths of lifespan of the inhabitants, the universal characteristic is that there are long 'ferries' of defilement everywhere. Fortune and misfortune alternate, continuing in endless cycles. Experiencing suffering in various modes of life, beings are long misled by four perverse views. Whether in causal acts or in resultant states, falsehood ensues. How detestable! For this reason, the Pure Land does not belong to the three worlds."[227]

Master Tao-ch'o, *An-le-chi (Anrakushu)*

*

"The reward of the Pure Land is free of desires, so it does not belong to the world of desire."[228]

Master Tao-ch'o quoting *Great Wisdom Discourse* in his *An-le-chi (Anrakushu)*

*

---

[226] *Kyogyoshinsho – On Teaching, Practice, Faith, and Enlightenment*, translated by Hisao Inagaki, Numata Center for Buddhist Translation and Research, Kyoto, 2003, p. 173

[227] *Collection of Passages on the Land of Peace and Bliss - AN LE CHI* by Tao-ch'o, translated by Zuio Hisao Inagaki, Horai Association International, Singapore, 2015, p 30-31.

[228] *Idem*, p 31.

135

"It is comforting and refreshing, and there are no seasonal changes."[229]

Master Tao-ch'o quoting *Hymns on the Larger Sutra [Hymn in Praise of Amida Buddha]* in his *An-le-chi (Anrakushu)*

*

"It is stated in the Pure Salvation Bodhisattva Sutra:

'If a man is mindful of Amida Buddha for ten years or five years, or for many years, he will be born in the land of infinite life; namely, he will attain the Dharma-body in the Pure Land, which is as inexhaustible and inconceivable as the sand-grains of the Ganges River.'[230]

In this defiled world, one's life-span is short; the karmic reward in this life soon ends. If you are born in Amida's Pure Land, your life-span[231] *will be long and inconceivable. [...]*

Each one of you should weigh this great benefit and should aspire to go there.

Master Tao-ch'o, *An-le-chi (Anrakushu)*

*

"We urge people to turn to the West for refuge. Once born there, the three learnings spontaneously advance and ten thousand practices are completely accomplished. Hence, the Larger Sutra states (adapted):

'In Amida's Pure Land, there is not even a place, as small as a hair's breadth, where evil is committed.'[232]

---

[229] *Idem*, p 32

[230] *Idem*, p.122

[231] Lifespan in the Pure Land refers to the transcendent bodies of those born in the Pure Land. Such a body will have no end. Accordingly, he can manifest freely in all the worlds to save sentient beings.

136

Master Tao-ch'o, *An-le-chi (Anrakushu)*

*

"After having reached the Pure Land, you will acquire the six supernatural powers, with which you enter Samsara and guide sentient beings in all future ages".[233]
Master Shan-tao, *Ojoraisan*

*

"I wish to abandon the body enclosed in the womb
And attain birth in the Land of Peace and Bliss,
Where I will quickly behold Amida Buddha's
Body of boundless merits and virtues
And see many Tathagathas
And holy sages as well.
Having acquired the six supernatural powers,
I will continue to save suffering sentient beings
Until all their worlds throughout the universe are exhausted.
Such will be my vow.
After having thus made a vow, I take refuge in Amida Buddha
with sincerity of heart". [234]
Master Shan-tao, Ojoraisan

*

"All of the teachings that enable one to accomplish Buddhahood in this defiled world of suffering are called the Holy Gate. To realize Enlightenment through contemplating the true nature of all existence; to pursue purification of the six sensory organs through meditating

---

[232] *Collection of Passages on the Land of Peace and Bliss - AN LE CHI* by Tao-ch'o, translated by Zuio Hisao Inagaki, Horai Association International, Singapore, 2015, p.127

[233] *Shan-tao's Liturgy for Birth – Ojoraisan*, compiled by Master Shan-tao, annotated translation by Zuio Hisao Inagaki, edited by Doyi Tan, Singapore, 2009, p.38

[234] *Idem*, 2009, p.68

exclusively on the Lotus Sutra; to aspire to the realization of Buddhahood in one's very existent state through the observance of the three mystic practices; to pursue the four paths to achieve Nirvana; to aspire to attainment of the three transcendent faculties and the six transcendent faculties – these are called the difficult path.

In contrast, **the teaching of the Pure Land gate begins with the attainment of birth in the Pure Land in the first place, followed by the realization of Enlightenment and Buddhahood there** *– this is called the easy path".*[235]

Honen Shonin, *Wago Toroku*

*

"If they are born into the Pure Land they are endowed with a superior wisdom and their clear power of mysterious communication reaches unto those who were formerly their benefactors and to those who were their acquaintances through many lives and generations, they can attract them freely. Endowed with a heavenly eye, they can see where they live, and with their heavenly ear they can hear their voice. Their wisdom of destiny enables them to remember the favors (of their former benefactors) and with their insight into others' hearts they understand their hearts. Their mysterious powers of communication enable them to go where they are, and by changing their form they can adapt themselves to their needs and in various ways teach them and lead them in
the way of salvation.

And again it is explained in the Byodokyo where we read: "Those who are born in the Pure Land of the West know for themselves where they lived in their previous lives, what was their state and by what causes they are now born into the Pure Land. Since they know everything about the present state of every being that goes and come to and from the Eight Directions and up and down, they understand

---

[235] *The Promise of Amida Buddha: Honen's Path to Bliss* – the first English translation of the Genko edition of the works of Honen Shonin composed in Japanese - also known as *Collected Teachings of Kurodani Shonin: The Japanese Anthology (Wago Toroku)*, translated by Joji Atone and Yoko Hayashi, Wisdom Publications, Boston, 2011, p. 187-188

what the various heavenly beings, birds, beasts and insects think in their minds and the language which they speak."[236]

Master Genshin, *Ojoyoshu*

*

"What is called the pleasures of the First Opening of the Lotus is this: When a believer is born into the realm of the Pure Land we speak of it as the time of the First Opening of his Lotus. All his pleasures are increased a hundred thousand times above what they were before. Such a one is like a blind man who has for the first time received his sight, or like a man from the country who has suddenly been transported to a palace. As he looks at his own body his skin becomes radiant with golden rays. His clothes are made of natural treasures. Gold rings, hair ornaments of beautiful feathers, a crown of gems, a necklace of most wonderful jewels and such ornaments beyond description in their beauty, cover his body. As he beholds the radiance of the Buddha, his eyes become purified and he is able to see the multitudes that assemble in the next world and to hear the voice of the various Laws. Everything of form and sound is mysterious and marvelous

to him. When he looks up into the spacious sky he beholds a wide radiance of sublimity so glorious that heart and words cannot express it, and his eyes lose themselves in the path of clouds. The mysterious voice of the honorable Law is heard and it fills this Land of Treasures.

[...] The believers, while they were still in this evil world, could only read or hear about these things, but now they can see them for themselves. How great, then, must be their joy!"237

Master Genshin, *Ojoyoshu*

*

---

[236] *Genshin's Ojoyoshu – Collected Essays on Birth into the Pure Land*, translated from Japanese by A.K. Reischauer, The Transactions of the Asiatic Society of Japan, second series, volume VII, 1930, free online edition at http://www.amida-ji-retreat-temple-romania.blogspot.ro/2014/03/genshins-ojoyoshu-free-english-edition.html#more

[237] *Idem*

"The various beings of The Pure Land have all the five mysterious communications whose marvelous nature cannot be comprehended. They live a life of freedom according to their heart's desire. If, for example, they wish to look across the universe without taking a step they can do so. If they wish to hear the voice of anyone in the universe they can do so without moving

from their seats. Not only this, but they can hear also the things of the infinite past as if they were happening today. They know the inmost thoughts of the beings of the Six Realms as if they were reflected in a mirror. They can go and come freely as if all the lands of the Buddha in all the ten directions lay beneath their feet. They can do anything they please in the realm of infinite space and in the realm of endless time.

The forms of beings in this present evil world are thirty-two in number, and who is there that can obtain even one of these? But as for the Five Mysterious Communications, what kind of being is there that has attained even one! For beings in our world it is impossible to see without sun light or lamp-light; and, without moving, it is impossible to approach an object. We cannot see through even one sheet of paper. We know nothing of the things in the past; we know merely the things of the present moment. We are still confined to the cage and obstructed in every direction. But as for the beings in the Pure Land there is not one which does not have this power (of mysteriously transcending space and time). Even though for a period of a hundred Great Kalpas they have not planted the seed (karma) of the Special Characteristic Forms and have not created the cause for the Mysterious Communications, during the Four Meditations, they still have this power as a natural consequence of having been born into the Pure Land. How happy, then, they must be!"[238]

Master Genshin, *Ojoyoshu*

*

---

[238] Idem

"As they have power to understand their own destinies, they talk to each other about their former lives, namely, as to what country they lived in, how their mind became enlightened by this and that scripture when they were seeking the way of the Buddha, how they kept this and that precept,

and learned such and such teachings and thus developed the Good Root, and how they gave such and such alms. In this way they talk with one another about the virtues which they enjoyed, or they tell in detail the story from beginning to end of how they came to be born into the Pure Land."[239]

Master Genshin, *Ojoyoshu*

*

"They will recite the entire canon in a moment and explain most perfectly the most profound passages. Thus their enjoyment continues without any interruption. Their place is a place of incorruption, and in this pure Land of Pleasure they abide forever and thus have for all time escaped from the terrors of the Three Realms and the Eight Difficulties[240]. Life here is boundless and their state is not subject to birth and death, nor do they endure the four sufferings of birth, old age, sickness and death which characterize human life.

[...] Their body is as of diamond and so is not burned even though it is in fire. It does

not become tarnished even though it is in the mud. Their heart is not stained with the dust of their environment. Their marvelous body of purity and strength is not affected by the sufferings of any and all

---

[239] *Idem*

[240] The Eight Difficulties are: 1. Blindness and Deafness, 2. Worldly Wisdom (because tempted by it), 3. Being born before or after a Buddha appears in the world, 4. Happiness in Hokurashu (a pleasant land in China. One becomes so engrossed with the pleasures in this land that one fails to listen to the Buddha and so misses eternal life, 5. the Happiness of long life on earth (since this keeps one from Buddha's salvation), 6. Existence in Hell, 7. Existence in the Realm of Hungry Spirits, 8 Existence in the Realm of Beasts.

sufferings combined[241]. They are never injured even though attacked by ten times ten thousand numberless warriors armed with spears and arrows. They are not burned even though they may be in the midst of limitless flames; nor are they drowned though they are submerged in a fathomless ocean. Therefore they can go freely even into the eight Hot Hells and the eight Cold Hells in order to save their relatives from the Three Worlds and the Six Realms.

[...] There is nothing but suffering when we examine even the smallest parts of our bodies, not to mention the larger parts. But when we have been born into this Pure Land everything is like a diamond changeless, permanent, without increase or decrease, wonderful, and therefore there is no such suffering as in our fleshly body; yea, it is less than the finest particle of dust."[242]

Master Genshin, *Ojoyoshu*

*

„The monks and laity of this latter age and the religious teachers of these times are floundering in concepts of ‚self-nature' and ‚mind only', and they disparage the true realization of Enlightenment in the Pure Land way".[243]

Shinran Shonin, *Kyogyoshinsho*, chapter III

*

"It is stated in the Collection of Passages on the Land of Peace and Bliss (An le chi):

---

[241] Sufferings combined. This is the eight of the Eight Difficulties, namely: 1. Birth, 2. Old Age, 3. Sickness, 4. Death, 5. Hatred, 6. Separation, 7. Frustration of one's desire, 8. The combination of the preceding seven sufferings.

[242] *Genshin's Ojoyoshu – Collected Essays on Birth into the Pure Land*, translated from Japanese by A.K. Reischauer, The Transactions of the Asiatic Society of Japan, second series, volume VII, 1930, free online edition at http://www.amida-ji-retreat-temple-romania.blogspot.ro/2014/03/genshins-ojoyoshu-free-english-edition.html#more

[243] *The Collected Works of Shinran*, Shin Buddhism Translation Series, Jodo Shinshu Hongwanji-ha, Kyoto, 1997, p.77

The Sutra on the Buddha-Contemplation Samâdhi (Buddhadhyana-samadhi-sutra) says:

[Shakyamuni] urged his father, the king (Suddhodana), to practice the Nembutsu samadhi. His father, the king, asked the Buddha, "Why do you not recommend to me, your disciple, the practice of meditating on the ultimate virtue of the Buddha's stage, which is identical with true Suchness, ultimate reality, or the highest principle of emptiness (Sunyata)?"

The Buddha answered his father, the king, "The ultimate virtue of the Buddhas is the boundless and profoundly subtle state and is possessed of transcendent faculties and the wisdom of liberation. This is not a state fit to be practiced by ordinary people. So I urge you, the king, to practice the Nembutsu samadhi."

His father, the king, asked the Buddha, "What are the characteristics of the merit of the Nembutsu?" The Buddha replied to his father, the king, "Suppose there is a forest of eranda trees, forty yojanas square, and there is in it a single cow-headed sandalwood tree, whose roots and sprouts are still underground. The eranda forest is full of a foul smell and completely devoid of pleasant scent. If someone bites a flower or fruit of the eranda tree, he will become insane and die. Later, when the sandalwood spreads its roots and buds and is about to grow into a tree, it emits luxuriant fragrance and finally transforms this forest into a sweet-smelling one. Those who see this are wonderstruck."

The Buddha said to his father, the king, "A thought of the Nembutsu that all sentient beings hold in birth and death is like this. If only one concentrates one's thought on the Buddha without interruption, one will surely be born in the presence of the Buddha. ***Once this person attains birth in the Pure Land, he will transform all the evils into great compassion, just as the fragrant sandalwood tree transforms the erada forest.***"

Here the eranda tree symbolizes the three poisons and the three hindrances within sentient beings and the innumerable grave karmic evils they commit. The sandalwood tree represents the thought of the

143

Nembutsu in sentient beings. "Is about to grow into a tree" shows that if only sentient beings keep practicing the Nembutsu without interruption, the karmic cause of their birth in the Pure Land is accomplished"[244].

*

"When ordinary beings reach the Western Land,
Their karmic evils, countless as particles, from long past kalpas will perish.
Endowed with the six supernatural powers, they attain unrestricted freedom in action;
Forever freed of old age and sickness, they are liberated from impermanence."[245]

The hymns by Fa-chao, based on the Sutra in Praise of the Pure Land (Sukhavativyuha), quoted by Shinran in his *Kyogyoshinsho*, chapter II.

*

"In the Western Land one advances in the Way more quickly than in this Saha world,
Because that land is free of the five desires and Adversaries".[246]

The hymns by Fa-chao based on the Sutra on the Life of the Buddha (Buddha-carita), quoted by Shinran Shonin in his *Kyogyoshinsho*, chapter II.

*

Foolish beings who have committed the ten evil acts and the five grave offenses
Have been drowning in samsara for eternally long kalpas,

---

[244] *Kyogyoshinsho – On Teaching, Practice, Faith, and Enlightenment*, translated by Hisao Inagaki, Numata Center for Buddhist Translation and Research, Kyoto, 2003, p. 29-30.
[245] *Idem*, p. 41-41.
[246] *Idem*, p. 42-43.

covered with the dust of evil passions.
When they reach Amida's land by calling his Name even
once,
They will become one with the Dharma-nature body.[247]
The hymns by Fa-chao based on the Sutra on Contemplation of
Amitayus (Contemplation Sutra), as quoted by Shinran Shonin in his
Kyogyoshinsho, chapter II

*

*"It is stated in the Teaching Assembly of the Tathagata of Infinite
Life:*
*'The people in the Pure Land are sages, and the land is
exquisite'.*[248]

It is also stated:
*In general, in order to make ordinary and inferior beings
increase their desire for birth, one should reveal the excellent
qualities of that land.*[249]
Shinran Shonin, *Kyogyoshinsho*, chapter II

*

Master Yüan-chao says:
*The way of destroying delusion and realizing true suchness
in this world, which is based on one's self-power, is expounded
in various Mahayana and Hinayana sutras. The way of realizing
enlightenment after going to another land and hearing
the Dharma there is necessarily dependent on the Other-
Power, and so birth in the Pure Land is taught.*[250]
Shinran Shonin, *Kyogyoshinsho*, chapter II

*

---

[247] *Idem*, p. 45.
[248] *Idem*, p. 47.
[249] *Idem*, p. 48.
[250] *Idem*, p. 65.

Upon reaching the Lotus-store world,
We will realize true Suchness and attain the Dharma body.
Then, playing in the forests of evil passions, we will display
supernatural powers;
Entering samsaric states, we will manifest accommodated
and transformed bodies to save beings.[251]
Shinran Shonin, *Hymns of True Faith and Nembutsu (Shoshin
nembutsu ge)*
Kyogyoshinsho, chapter II

*

"*Concerning birth in the Pure Land, the Larger Sutra says, 'They
are all endowed with bodies of naturalness, emptiness, and infinity'.
The Discourse on the Pure Land states, 'The hosts of sages in the
likeness of pure flowers surrounding the Tathagata are born there,
transformed from within the flower of enlightenment'. Also the
Commentary on Vasubandhu's Discourse on the Pure Land says,
'They are so born by one and the same path of the Nembutsu, and not
by other paths.' Also it is said, 'Inconceivable birth.'*"[252]
Shinran Shonin, *Kyogyoshinsho*, chapter V

*

"*When a person realizes the mind of nondiscrimination,*
*That attainment is the 'state of regarding each being as one's only
child'.*
This is none other than Buddha-nature;
We will awaken to it on reaching the land of peace.

> *Tathagata is non other than Nirvana;*
> *Nirvana is called Buddha-nature.*
> *Beyond our ability to attain it in the state of foolish beings,*

---

[251] *Idem*, p. 78.
[252] *Idem*, p. 231

146

We will realize it on reaching the Land of Peace."[253]
Shinran Shonin, *Hymns of the Pure Land (Jodo Wasan)*

*

"If not for the Buddha's directing of virtue,
How could we realize Enlightenment in the Pure Land?"[254]
Shinran Shonin, *Hymns of the Dharma- Ages (Koso Wasan)*

*

In the *Essentials of Faith Alone* by Master Seikaku, it is said:
"'The Land of Bliss is the realm of Nirvana, the uncreated'.[255]

Here is the comment of Shinran:

"'The Land of Bliss' is that Pure Land of happiness, where there
are always countless joys and never any suffering mingled with them.
It is known as the Land of Peace. It was Master T'an-luan who
praised it and called it 'Land of Peace'. Also, the Treatise on the
Pure Land describes it as 'the Lotus Repository World' and as the
uncreated.*
*'The realm of Nirvana' refers to the place where one overturns the
delusion of ignorance and realizes the supreme Enlightenment.
'Realm' means 'place'; know it as the place of attaining
Enlightenment.*'"[256]
Shinran Shonin, *Notes on Essentials of Faith Alone*

*

Commenting on the words of Honen, *"Namo Amida Butsu: as the*
act that leads to birth in the Pure Land, the nembutsu is taken to be
fundamental", Shinran said:

---

[253] *The Collected Works of Shinran*, Shin Buddhism Translation Series, Jodo
Shinshu Hongwanji-ha, Kyoto, 1997, p. 350.
[254] *Idem*, p. 411.
[255] *Idem*, p. 460.
[256] *Idem*, p. 460-461.

147

"Know that these words proclaim the right cause of birth in the Pure Land of peace to be none other than the nembutsu. 'Right cause' is the seed for being born in the Pure Land and unfailingly attaining Buddhahood".[257]

Shinran Shonin, *Notes on the Inscriptions on Sacred Scrolls*

*

"And so, as Shakyamuni has taught, at the very moment that we, possessed of ignorance and blind passions, are born into the Pure Land of peace, we attain the supreme fruit of Buddhahood."[258]

Shinran Shonin, *Lamp for the Latter Ages*, Letter 2 – Response to an Inquiry from the Nembutsu People of Kasama.

*

"Nirvana is perfect Enlightenment. T 'an-luan's commentary tells of a tree called 'great firmness'. This tree lies buried underground for one hundred years, but when it sends forth shoots, it grows one hundred yards a day. Just as the tree spends one hundred years underground, we abide in this Saha world in the stage of the truly settled. And just as it grows one hundred yards in a single day, such is our attainment of Nirvana."[259]

Shinran Shonin, *Lamp for the Latter Ages*, Letter 14

*

"When a person has entered completely into the Pure Land of happiness, he or she immediately realizes the supreme Nirvana; he realizes the supreme Enlightenment. Although the terms differ, they both mean to realize the Enlightenment of the Buddha who is

---

[257] *Idem*, p. 512.
[258] *Idem*, p. 526.
[259] *Idem*, p. 544.

148

Dharma-body [ultimate Dharmakaya]. This is known as directing virtue for the sake of our going forth in Birth.[260]
Shinran Shonin, *Lamp for the Latter Ages*, Letter 21

*

"Pure, wondrous, without bound is Amida's land,
And possessed of great adornments;
The different virtues all reach fulfillment there -
It excels all Buddha-lands of the ten quarters.[261]
Shinran Shonin, *Passages on the Pure Land Way*

*

"The first is karmic power; [the land] has been fulfilled
By the karmic power of Dharmakara's great Vow.
The second is the power of the good of Amida,
The perfectly enlightened Dharma-king, by which [the land] is embraced."

Unlike our world, which appeared due to the collective karma of beings born here, the Pure Land is the effect of the *karmic power of Dharmakara's great Vow.* Thus, the Pure Land is not here and now, in this samsaric world.

"We necessarily attain birth in the Land of Happiness,
And thereupon realize that birth and death is itself great Nirvana.
This is the path of easy practice; it is termed Other Power.

On reaching the Land of Happiness, necessarily,
by the spontaneous working of the Vow,
Such a person immediately attains the eternal bliss of dharma-
nature."[262]
Shinran Shonin, *Hymns of the Two Gateways*

---

[260] *Idem*, p. 555.
[261] *Idem*, p. 304.
[262] *Idem*, p. 628-629.

*

"Concerning the directing of virtue through the power of the Primal Vow, the Tathagata's directing of virtue has two aspects: the directing of virtue in the aspect for our going forth to the Pure Land and the directing of virtue in the aspect for our return to this world."[263]

Shinran Shonin, *Passages on the Two Aspects of the Tathagata's Directing of Virtue*

*

"Because of the true cause – Amida Tathagata's directing of virtue for our going forth – we realize the enlightenment of supreme Nirvana. This is the true intent of the Larger Sutra. Hence, it is termed "birth in accord with the Larger Sutra," and also "birth that is inconceivable."[264]

Shinran Shonin, *A Collection of Passages on the Types of Birth in the Pure Land Sutras*

*

"Question: Should we understand the state of being truly settled and that of Nirvana as one benefit, or as two?

Answer: The dimension of 'the awakening of the one thought-moment of shinjin' is that of joining the company of those truly settled'. This is the benefit we gain in the defiled world. Next, it should be understood that Nirvana is the benefit to be gained in the Pure Land. Hence we should think of them as two benefits".[265]

Rennyo Shonin, *Letters*

---

[263] *Idem*, p. 628-633.

[264] *Idem*, p. 628-639.

[265] *Rennyo Shonin Ofumi: The Letters of Rennyo*, translated from the Japanese (Taisho, Volume 74, Number 2668) by Ann T. Rogers and Minor L. Rogers, Numata Center for Buddhist Translation and Research, Berkeley, California, 1996, p.14

*

"The human realm is a place of uncertainty. The Land of Utmost Bliss is one of eternity. Hence we should not make our abode in the uncertain human realm, but rather aspire to birth in the eternal Land of Utmost Bliss. In our tradition, therefore, the matter of faith is placed before all else; unless we are fully aware of the reason for this, everything is meaningless. We must promptly undergo a decisive settling of faith (anjin) and aspire to birth in the Pure Land."[266]

Rennyo Shonin, *Letters*

---

[266] *Idem*, p.115

**This book was printed from
the donations sent by people in this list:**

Jonathan Khor – *"on behalf of the deceased Mr. Loh Khin Kok and Ms. Teh Phek Hong. May the merits gained adorn Amitabha's Pure Land, and be dedicated to all sentient beings. May they all be reborn in the Pure Land"*

Richard Fairley (Jiyu)
Che'usa Wend - *"in the memory of my parents, Bill and Phyllis Stoner"*
Neal Oldham
Carmen Ramos
Veronica Anghelescu
Cristian Anton
Jeremiah Mullica
Kenya-Lee Province
Steve Bastasch

Printed in Great Britain
by Amazon